DH82 Tiger Moth elementary trainer, long-distance flyer – David Cyster's Moth on its return from Australia

Right Familiar tractor tug

SCENE ON THE GROUND

A 'flying day' at Old Warden aerodrome provides a unique opportunity to see many of the Shuttleworth Collection's vintage aircraft in action. My drawing depicts a typical scene.

The Hawker Hind receives attention while the Gloster Gladiator prepares to leave the flight line. Overhead the Fairey Swordfish visits from her base with the Royal Navy Historic Flight at Yeovilton.

Right   Republic P47 Thunderbolt at Duxford

SCENE ON THE GROUND

An artist's view of historic aircraft

EVAN IVORY

Castlemead
PUBLICATIONS

WELWYN GARDEN CITY

First Published in 1991

CASTLEMEAD PUBLICATIONS
12 Little Mundells
Welwyn Garden City
Hertfordshire, AL7 1EW

Proprietors: Ward's Publishing Services

ISBN 0 948555 25 4

Text and illustrations © Evan Ivory, 1990

British Library Cataloguing in Publication Data
Ivory, Evan
  Scene on the ground.
  1. Aircraft, to 1976 – Illustrations
  I. Title
  629.1330904

ISBN 0-948555-25-4

Phototypeset in 12pt Palatino Roman Type
by Intype, London
Printed in Great Britain by
Eagle Colourbooks, Blantyre

Acknowledgements

The author wishes to thank the following people for kindly granting him permission to draw, or special access to, the aircraft:

David Cyster RAF (Rtd) and Cherry Cyster
Terry Pankhurst and David Wingate, British Aerospace
Toni Bianchi, Personal Plane Services
Mrs J. S. Scivyer, The Mosquito Aircraft Museum
Peter Rushen, The Imperial War Museum (Duxford)
Members of staff at the Shuttleworth Trust, The Fleet Air Arm Museum, The Royal Air Force Museum and Air Vice Marshall W. J. Wrattan, AFC, Air Officer commanding 11 Group.

Museums and Collections from which the majority of the drawings originated

The Shuttleworth Collection, Old Warden Aerodrome, near Biggleswade, Beds, SG18 9ER
The Royal Air Force Museum, Hendon, London, NW9 5LL
The Science Museum, South Kensington, London, SW7 2DD
Booker Aircraft Museum, Booker Airfield, High Wycombe, Bucks. HP11 2JZ
The Fleet Air Arm Museum, RNAS, Yeovilton, Somerset, BA22 8HT
Mosquito Aircraft Museum, Box 107, Salisbury Hall, London Colney, St Albans, Herts, AL2 1BU
The Imperial War Museum (Duxford), Duxford Airfield, Duxford, Cambridge, CB2 4QR
(A number of aircraft at the Duxford site are on loan from private collections or groups such as Plain Sailing Displays, The Fighter Collection and The Old Flying Machine Company. The author is pleased to include a number of these aircraft in his drawings.)
   He wishes to thank Richard Riding, Editor of *Aeroplane Monthly*, and Temple Press for permission to use the extract from *Guide to Flying*, and Derrick Ballington, Chief Librarian, Janes Information Group, for permission to use the extract from *The Spitfire Story*.
   Grateful thanks are also due to his friends Charles Roberts, Bob Cutts and Christopher Cutts for their encouragement and practical help, and to the British Library for help with researching technical information.
   Finally the author would like to thank Susan King for her constructive help and patience in the preparation of the text and the staff of Castlemead Publications for all their kindness.

Contents

W4050. The De Havilland Mosquito prototype now resides at Salisbury Hall, near St Albans, where it was designed and built. (This has since become the Mosquito Museum.) The first aircraft was taken by road to nearby Hatfield aerodrome where it made its maiden flight on 25th November 1940.

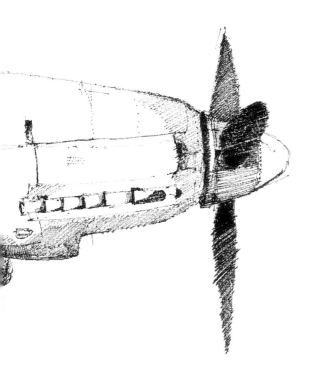

Images of war. To my eye the Junkers JU87 is the definitive image of war. With its angular tail and cranked wings in contrast to the seductive taper of the rear fuselage, it is both arresting and unforgettable. My drawing was made from the gallery at the Royal Air Force Museum. Originally an 87D–5, the machine was later modified to JU87G standard by the removal of the dive brakes and the addition of mounting points for two 37mm BK 3.7 guns.

The figure in the cockpit detail is the visitor from the USA to whom I refer in the Introduction.

Below Another image of war, the Boulton Paul Defiant lacks the satanic overtones of the Junkers. As I drew it I was reminded faintly of the Hurricane. However, where the Hurricane is very handsome the Defiant is not, the turret breaking the line of its back. The tail fin is angular and seemingly unfinished.

The type is particularly remembered for its night-fighting role during the Blitz of 1940–41.

Close company. Within the confines of a crowded hangar it is often impossible to get a clear view of one single aircraft. Sometimes the overlapping of shapes provides a pleasing composition. Here the Sopwith Pup (1916) and the Bristol F 2b (1917) reflect on times past.

Memories and Introductions

My childhood was spent near two airfields, both famous, De Havilland at Hatfield and Handley Page at Radlett. I am convinced in retrospect that this has much to do with my enthusiasm for drawing aircraft.

I recall during my school days the almost matter-of-fact way I would record aircraft passing over our Hertfordshire home – the Tiger Moths practising aerobatics and low-flying over fields where I picnicked with my parents.

The Mosquito made a big impact as it roared over the house, banking steeply to dive out of sight onto the aerodrome at Hatfield. I would note the changes as the different versions screamed over; the perspex nose of the bomber, later with the bulged bomb bay, the fighter variant and the PR machine – all were mentally noted in meticulous detail. A more imaginative enemy might have instructed his spies in the art of making friends with the young: a schoolboy could have provided endless titbits as he ate through his bag of Smiths crisps!

The Handley Page Halifax bombers test-flying from the Radlett site were more discreet; they would cruise over at low altitude heading towards the aerodrome; presumably on test, they were unarmed and not anxious to meet up with a lurking enemy. I recall noting the enlarged tail fin of the later version Halifax on test quite early on. Recently, I met a 'Halifax man' who had worked on the type. Apparently my childhood memories are correct. They were the Mk III fitted with radial engines. Confirmation at last!

Then of course there was the unforgettable sight one Sunday morning (September 17 1944) of hundreds of gliders with their tugs. They passed endlessly overhead. I have since read that Hatfield was a marshalling point for the great aerial armada to Arnhem, code named 'Market Garden'. My father and I knew nothing of this at the time. We just stood and watched in wonderment.

After the war, my uncle took me (on the pillion of his 500cc AJS motorcycle) to Radlett to see an eye-opening full-blooded air display. The event, which became an annual delight for me, was, of course, the Display and Exhibition of the Society of British Aircraft Constructors, later to move from the home of Handley Page in Hertfordshire to its present venue at Farnborough, Hants. There were many interesting aircraft to see in those days when the Spitfire and Mosquito shared the stage with the 'new' machines, Vampires, Meteors and exciting experimental machines such as the de Havilland 108 Swallow, a futuristic tail-less experimental type, but for me the excitement was added to because one could actually see aeroplanes take off and land: to this day I have a picture of a Handley Page Hermes bouncing along the runway as the hapless pilot tried to stick it on the tarmac; if there was a commentator present, I have no doubt he yielded to the temptation to remark on the number of landing fees the pilot would expect to pay! (In fairness to the gentleman at the controls, he had but two huge main wheels with which to 'get it right', unlike his counterparts of today, whose machines have multiple wheels to cushion their landing.)

When my turn for freedom came around after the customary two years' National Service, I opted for local release from BAOR. This meant that I could be demobbed in Germany and avoid coming home only to stagnate in a holding camp in the UK. Imagine my surprise and delight to board an Airspeed Ambassador for the flight home. What a beautiful twin-engined airliner this was. Interestingly the type had its origins in de Havilland and later passed to Airspeed. (I thought I recognised the cigar-like fuselage!) This was in the mid-1950s, when Heathrow was fenced with chestnut paling to prevent the viewing public from getting too close to the aircraft parked on the apron!

After the rigidity of Service life (I was once ordered to provide paintings for an art exhibition!), we chose Cornwall for a holiday, and while we were there a visit to the Scilly Isles was made all the more memorable by our transport –

'On the deck'. One of my vivid memories of World War II is of low-flying aircraft. Gone before the sound of their engines reached my ear, they were breathtaking. The sketch captures a moment as Blenheim IVs cross Hertfordshire countryside.

a beautiful de Havilland Rapide operated by the then British European Airways. On one of these flights we flew through a shower of rain. The pilot was quite unmoved as small streams of water flowed down the inside of his windscreen!

During my spell as a Lecturer in art and design I liked to encourage my students in the traditional practice of drawing. One day, with this in mind, I took a group on a visit to the famous Shuttleworth Collection at Old Warden, Bedfordshire. I found the aircraft there quite irresistible and decided to teach by example rather than lecture. I have no idea if I succeeded in passing on any useful information to the students, but at least I had a great day!

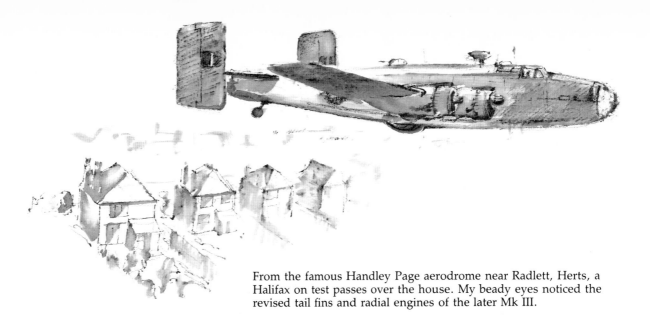

From the famous Handley Page aerodrome near Radlett, Herts, a Halifax on test passes over the house. My beady eyes noticed the revised tail fins and radial engines of the later Mk III.

The drawing I made that day – of a Gloster Gladiator – was the first of my drawings of an aircraft, and those that occupy most of this book are a sample of the many I have made since – drawings of aeroplanes that for whatever reason have caught my imagination and filled me with a desire to draw them. They are, thus, a mixed bag. Following no specific sequence, they typify my approach, to record what I see as it appeals. I have no desire to produce a chronicled history. It is simply a folio of drawings.

The point of my brief text is to explain my preoccupation with the tension between the technical and the visual; to comment on the engineering design and to suggest that much of the appeal to me lies in my emotional response to this. Further, to offer the point that designers of past decades had an instinctive eye; because I am an artist, I am concerned with aircraft as objects, pieces of machinery seen as structural forms, and I sense that this was, in part, how their designers too perceived them.

My aircraft are all from the pre-computer days. They stem from the efforts of the human brain. The labour of calculations and technical data was there of course, but the 'broad pencil' approach determined how it would look. And it shows. I am intrigued by a reference to this in Dr Alfred Price's definitive history *The Spitfire Story*. It makes the point better than I can.

> At this time aircraft design depended largely on what the chief designer and his team thought 'looked right'. On Mitchells's way of doing things, his chief designer Joe Smith, later wrote: 'He was an inveterate drawer of drawings, particularly general arrangements. He would modify the lines of an aircraft with the softest pencil he could find and then re-modify over the top with progressively thicker lines until one would finally be faced with a new outline of lines about three-sixteenths of an inch thick. But the results were always worthwhile, and the centre of the line was usually accepted when the thing was re-drawn.'

I have often heard the expression when referring to a good machine 'it is a pilot's aeroplane'. My folio is made up of drawings of my favourites. They are artists' aeroplanes! I draw, with few exceptions, from sight. This, I find, gives me a much greater intimacy with my subject than using photographs, though these are useful as back-ups. Being on site allows me to walk up to an aircraft and examine it in detail at first hand. However, it also has another attraction, and one which I value. Perched on my diminutive stool, I am often aware that I am being observed. I sense a presence behind my shoulder. At some point a gentle voice will say something like 'I used to work on those' – and then a conversation will follow which for me at least is always a pleasure and worth the hold-up to my work. I learn about aircraft this way – not facts or statistics, but what they were like to service and fly.

Occasionally I have a treat, as I did when I was drawing Plane Sailings' Catalina flying boat at Duxford airfield. An engineer had been toiling on the craft for some hours. (So had I – it's a difficult type to draw!) After a time he came over and asked if I would like a closer look. What a thrill to be invited aboard, to sit in the cockpit and peer out through the windscreen! As I looked up and out over my shoulders, the huge twin radial engines looked massive – the 'Cat' is a magnificent display aircraft!

Mosquito B35. TA 634 was in open storage among the rose beds
when I made the drawing on which this painting is based; dedicated
as a memorial to Group Capt. P. C. Pickard, it was coded EGE, the
code of No. 487 Squadron, who took part in the famous Amiens
prison raid, known as Operation Jericho. The Mosquito has now
undergone a superb restoration for static display within the museum
at Salisbury Hall.

It is not only British aircraft that attract attention and not just Britons that visit air museums to renew World War II memories. I remember an American pilot who had himself flown the B24 Liberator bomber who came over to me while I was drawing the JU87 Stuka dive-bomber. On seeing again this awesome war machine he remarked 'It looks smaller now! When you have one of those things coming at you with cannons firing' he went on 'it sure looks a big plane!' He was off to Scotland the next day in search of a 'meadow' where he force-landed a B24 during the war. I hope he found it!

It may take me two hours or so to complete a drawing, so I am aware of people coming and going. It was while I was drawing the Stuka that I met another enthusiast. He spent so much time around the machine, I drew him in my sketch! He drooled over it, jaw dropping open in sheer wonderment. Finally he obtained permission to sit in the cockpit, a rare privilege. Removing his shoes, he stepped carefully onto the wing, slid back the canopy and climbed aboard. I thought he would have to be forcibly extracted! Afterwards he told me he was building a 6/10th scale model of the machine in which he intends to fly and had come over from the States to get his hands on the real thing. They have an example over there, but it hangs from the roof of a gallery.

One privilege for me has been to visit Hatfield aerodrome (now part of British Aerospace). By kind arrangements with friends I have drawn a number of famous aircraft on this site. I first drew the DH Rapide G-AIYR at Hatfield while it was being prepared for use by David and Cherry Cyster. This couple flew to South Africa in imaginative commemoration of the pioneering long-distance flying achievements of Sir Alan Cobham. (In 1925 he flew to Cape Town and back; the following year he flew to Melbourne.) The Tiger Moth on the introductory page is the machine in which Squadron Leader David Cyster flew solo to Australia. Even in the late seventies and early eighties a flight of this distance is a major event. The Cysters' greatest reward for their efforts and skill was undoubtedly the successful accomplishment of their flying tribute to a great aviator of the past.

It was while I was drawing the DH88 Comet racer that I met two gentlemen working away on it as though it were just being prepared for the famous MacRobertson air race between Great Britain and Australia back in 1934. I talked to them as they perfected their latest 'mods' after the machine's magnificent restoration to flying condition. Imagine my surprise and thrill to learn that one of them had been tea boy at the Stag Lane site in 1934 and had seen the machine being built. Obviously, there are still a few details to be perfected, almost sixty years on!

I have a number of pilot friends with whom I can discuss aeroplanes. Among these is Bob Cutts, a close friend of very long standing, who during the war years flew Wellington and Stirling aircraft and was eventually shot down over the North Sea while on Special Operations flying the Stirling. He has many interesting stories to tell and one of my favourite relates to an early time in his career. It links his interest in flying with his passion for railways and recalls an episode with a DH82A Tiger Moth. He was at the time under intensive training with No. 7 Flying Training School Desford. Bob's story nicely rounds off my introduction to this book.

I was with a young Canadian (who had better remain nameless) and I was down for straight and level flying, climbing, gliding and stalling, and medium turns. He was a pleasant guy and I felt quite happy with him as I wrestled with the controls, overcorrecting like mad and wallowing around like a porpoise. Everybody knows how to fly an aeroplane but it's the feel you have to learn.

Anyway after a while he said 'OK feller, head for home now'. Well, I looked at the ground below and at the horizon without the slightest idea where 'home' was, and said 'Er, which way is it sir?' 'Shucks – I'm buffaloed myself – look for some smoke and I'll land someplace and ask' he replied.

Well, he decided on a field, rather a small one, I thought, with poplar trees on the approach side, but he sideslipped between them and was about to put the kite down when a chap with a horse and cart got in the way, so he opened up and had another look. We were now approaching an airfield with some Whitley bombers flying around, and he decided to go there (no radio and quite uninvited) so, the aerodrome control pilot pooped a red flare at us – so that was out.

Then he saw a long railway embankment with double track which was being widened to take two more tracks. The Pioneer Corps were working on it, it looked pretty level and was into the wind. So my Bush pilot of an instructor said he'd ask *them* the way! We took a slow precautionary pass along the embankment to inspect it and then decided to go in – the squaddies cleared out of the way quickly and he put us down on the ballast nicely – just as an LMS passenger train was overtaking us!

Sitting in the back seat with nothing to do I got a good view of their faces. A sergeant approached and he and my instructor went into a huddle over a map. One of the soldiers looked at me in the rear cockpit and said 'Is he your instructor?' 'Yes' says I, 'Struth!' said the soldier.

They pulled us back to give us enough take-off room and away we went. It was like taking off from an aircraft carrier and we dipped down into the valley as we went off the end but climbed up OK and he set course. 'OK you have control' he said, 'Keep on this heading and we should hit base in ten minutes.' 'Oh! by the way, I guess you won't report this – I'll see your time is OK!' The entry in my log says: 'Straight and level flying, climbing, gliding and stalling and medium turns' and it all lasted forty-five minutes.

Not everyone got to Arnhem on Sunday. A Horsa glider lands near a Hertfordshire village, having broken away from its Stirling tug.

The Wing

The Spitfire is both beautiful and unique. Proportioned to perfection its appearance has charisma and its attraction is unrivalled. It is unique in being identifiable in flight by almost everybody. You do not have to be an aircraft enthusiast to recognise it. The main reason for this instant recognition is of course its elliptical wings.

There is no better place for me to explain my fascination with aeroplanes than with the Spitfire, and in particular, the Spitfire's wings. I have studied the wing of a Spitfire from all angles. It has many subtleties, one of which is noticeable only from underneath – you have to examine a suspended machine to see it. There is a most sensitive blend of form, referred to as 'washout', where the trailing edge of the wing meets the fairing and blends into the fuselage. Technically this feature is brought about by the section of the wing, which is designed to have a twist of two and a half degrees from tip to root; apparently in tight turns the stall would start at the root of the wing before the tip, causing a judder to take place which gave the pilot warning of impending danger. For me, however, it simply presents great subtlety of form, and this I have tried to indicate in the diagram.

The plan form of the Spitfire's wings combines two principle features of advantage within the modest span of 36 feet 10 inches. Aerodynamically the elliptical shape allowed the wing to be thin. This was good since a thin wing produces less drag. It also provided sufficient room and strength to carry the guns and the undercarriage when retracted. However, Reginald Mitchell's chief designer Joe Smith admitted that along with its technical advantages the elliptical wing 'looked nice'. It is clear that an appreciation of beautiful forms is not the sole province of the artist!

Spitfire Mk IIa – a view I particularly like showing
the beautiful wing-root fairings. Drawn at RAF
Coningsby, P7350 belongs to The Battle of Britain
Memorial Flight. The machine was built at Castle
Bromwich and first flew in August 1940. After the
War it took part in the film *Battle of Britain*.

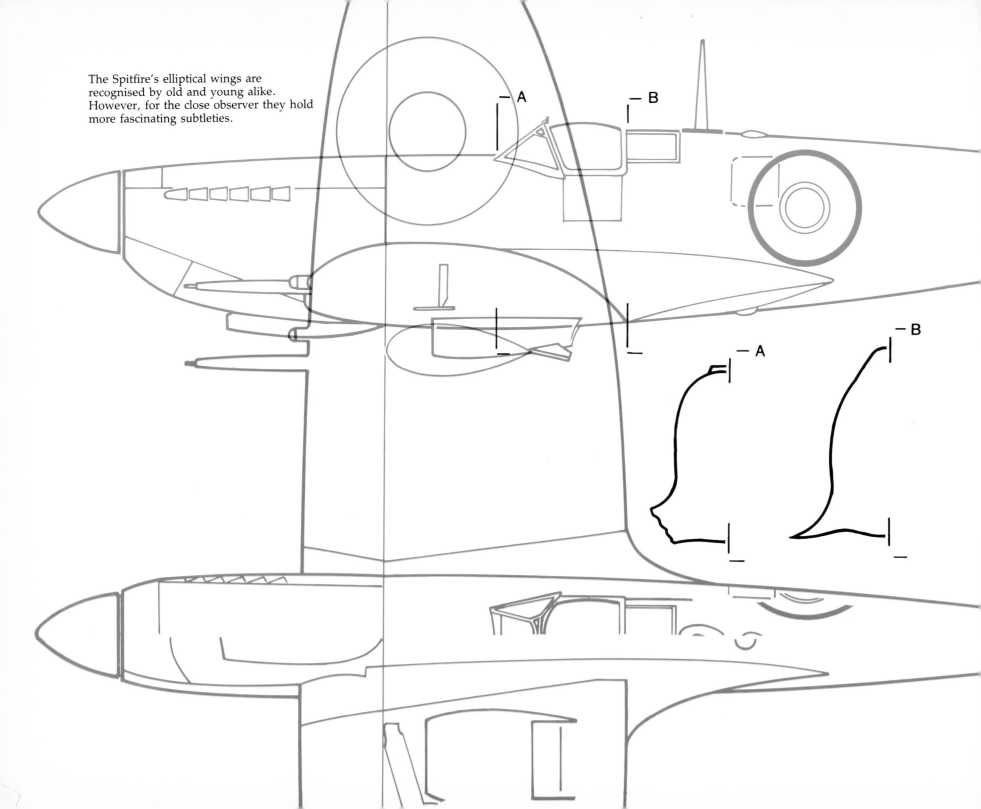

The Spitfire's elliptical wings are
recognised by old and young alike.
However, for the close observer they hold
more fascinating subtleties.

De Havilland Rapide

When I draw an aeroplane designed in the 1930s I can appreciate the beginnings of steamline forms. Often it is with details that one observes the care that designers took in an effort to obtain clean airflow. An aircraft which always delights me is the DH Rapide. As with the Spitfire, it has a beautiful wing plan with the control surfaces (ailerons) placed on the outer sections. Again it is the subtleties that attract me, subtleties such as the small fillets on the supporting struts between the upper and lower wings.

Since it is part traditional, and yet has such streamlined detail, I regard the Rapide as a transitional aeroplane – something old, something new. But the Avro Triplane of 1910 is very definitely an example of the former! With aeroplanes of this age the wings are very basic. Their ribs show through the fabric, countable as one draws them. Even when they are painted or doped and camouflaged the ribs cause the upper surface to ripple across its span. These ripples provide the artist with a visual account of the structure beneath. The struts and numerous wires are incomprehensible without some knowledge of their purpose; tracing them individually as they criss-cross before the eye, it is all too easy to have one or two to spare when the drawing is finished!

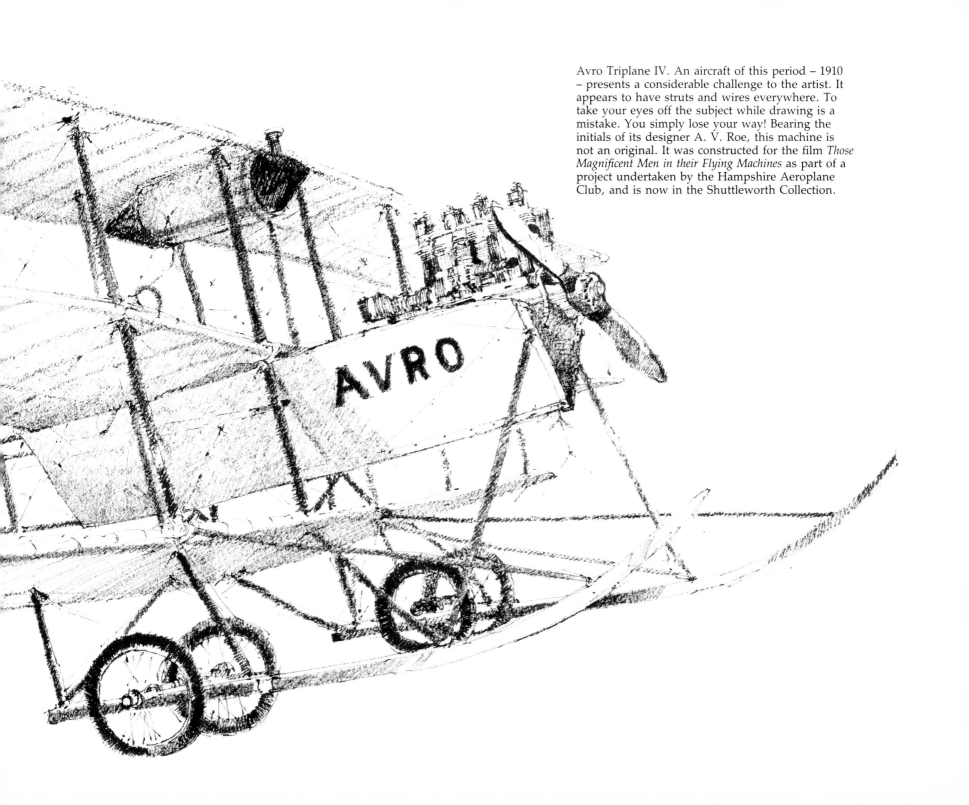

Avro Triplane IV. An aircraft of this period – 1910 – presents a considerable challenge to the artist. It appears to have struts and wires everywhere. To take your eyes off the subject while drawing is a mistake. You simply lose your way! Bearing the initials of its designer A. V. Roe, this machine is not an original. It was constructed for the film *Those Magnificent Men in their Flying Machines* as part of a project undertaken by the Hampshire Aeroplane Club, and is now in the Shuttleworth Collection.

The early wing is very basic in principle. The aileron had not been invented and the aeroplane was steered by means of 'warping' the wing – the surface of the entire structure could be moved differentially across its span. It is recorded, perhaps romantically, that the Wright brothers arrived at this means of control after watching buzzards soaring. My drawing of the Deperdussin shows an example of a type using the wing-warping method of lateral control. It is also of similar size to the machine used by Bleriot, the Type XI, for his historic crossing of the English Channel on 25th July 1909. When I draw one of these old machines, I can see how much drag must have been caused by all the paraphernalia of supports necessary to hold the wing in place.

By way of dramatic contrast we may at a glance look at a very different aircraft. One on which the wing has been reduced to an ultimate simplicity, the DH Comet. How do those slim wings stay in place? A technical description of this machine tells the story. Unlike earlier types here all is definitely not revealed. Not only have the bracing wires gone, the ribs too are invisible. In fact the wing has no visible means of support. It has no rivets; externally it is totally clean. It is a true cantilever of sandwich construction. A full description of the construction appeared in *The Aeroplane* of September 19 1934. It included an absorbing collection of articles brought together and republished in 1981 by IPC Business Press under the title *De Havilland – The Golden Years 1919 to 1939*. In the technical review Mr A. Hagg, the then works manager to the de Havilland company, explained that the wing got its strength from layers of narrow diagonal planking. This was laid over an internal structure of three spars, ribs and stringers. The Comet's success in the McRobertson Race from Mildenhall to Melbourne made it famous. It was a great pleasure to me to have had the opportunity of drawing it since its total restoration to flying condition; finished in its original livery – a really bright red with large registration letters in white – it looks every inch a racer.

Light and shade play an important part in the
appearance of an aircraft. Here, the Deperdussin of
1910 awaits its turn to leave the hangar for the flight
line at Old Warden aerodrome.

The beautifully restored Comet Racer receives constant and affectionate attention by two gentlemen having between them a very long association with the machine. I persuaded them to pose for me.

Out of the three Comets entered for the MacPherson Robertson air race in October 1934 between England and Australia, G-ACSS 'Grosvenor House' was the first to cross the finishing line. These striking aircraft were designed and built in nine months.

The dragonfly appearance of the Westland Lysander – its high wing has an unmistakable identity. This machine, a Mk III, was used on coastal patrol duties and reconnaissance work.

With the metal wing, I enjoy tracing the panels with those thousands of rivets, the construction around the bins where the undercarriage tucks up, small inspection panels, instructions for jacking, and so on. The ribs have long since disappeared from sight, but there remains much to look for and record.

The private owner of the 1930s would have appreciated the folding wing, a feature of particular advantage when space was at a premium; you could tow your plane behind the car and park it alongside in the garage. The ultimate yuppy! It is interesting to me that this principle was thought of and perfected so many years ago.

Since storage below deck is essential for aircraft operating from a carrier, types associated with seaborne operations are great fun to draw. The Corsair

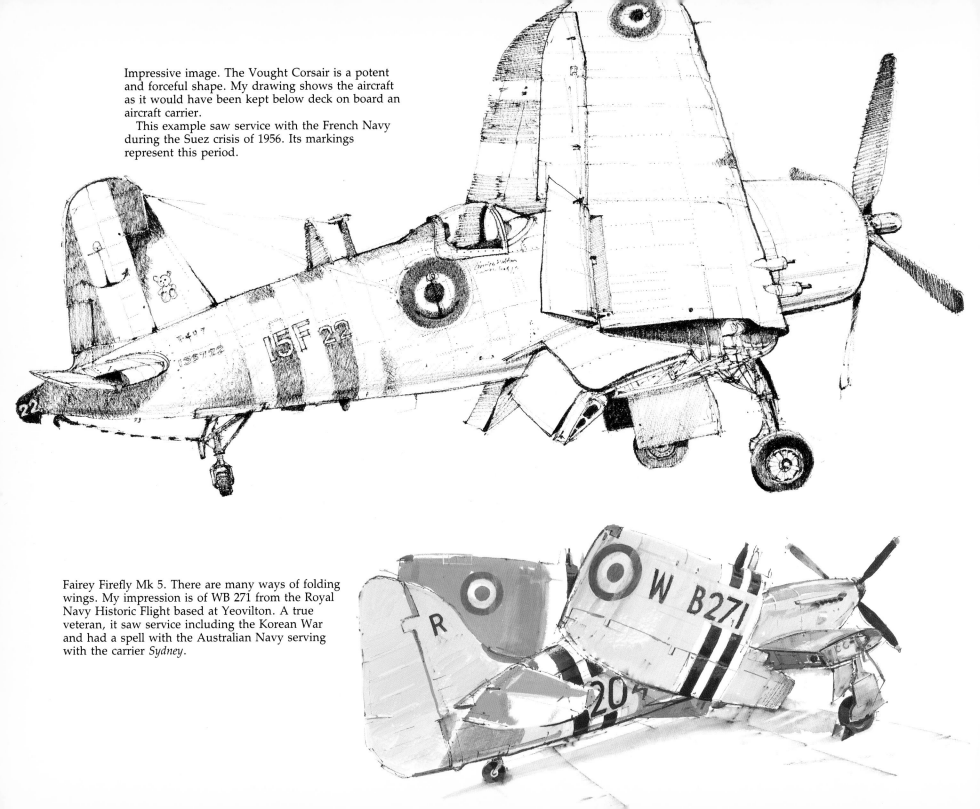

Impressive image. The Vought Corsair is a potent and forceful shape. My drawing shows the aircraft as it would have been kept below deck on board an aircraft carrier.

This example saw service with the French Navy during the Suez crisis of 1956. Its markings represent this period.

Fairey Firefly Mk 5. There are many ways of folding wings. My impression is of WB 271 from the Royal Navy Historic Flight based at Yeovilton. A true veteran, it saw service including the Korean War and had a spell with the Australian Navy serving with the carrier *Sydney*.

The Grumman Bearcat has the look of a high-performance racer. This aircraft served with the United States Navy from 1946 to 1948.

is a most distinctive shape, with its familiar cranked-wing design allowing the undercarriage to be placed at a low point and giving the machine good ground-clearance for its large propellor, and with its wings folded over the tubby fuselage giving it a predatory appearance.

Although I have suggested that most of the aircraft in my folio belong to the period when designers had an instinctive eye for getting things right, there are exceptions. The Gannet, cluttered with a mass of appendages and protruberances, is a challenge to draw; with its wings double-folded over its back and that arrestor hook protruding, sting-like, from under the tail, it looks like a predatory prehistoric insect encountered in a museum of natural history. I am tempted to ask how a machine looking like the Gannet could ever get off the ground. I recall sleepless nights on a holiday near Culdrose in Cornwall, Gannet's were flying circuits and bumps into the early hours and the noise from those Double Mamba turboprops nearly put me off aircraft for life! Not a beautiful machine but I enjoyed drawing it.

Moving into the jet age, we find the Sea Venom providing a contrasting

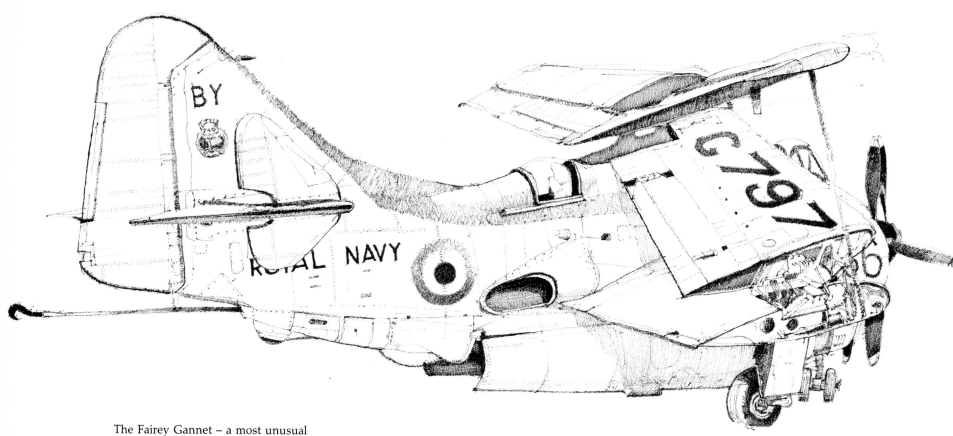

The Fairey Gannet – a most unusual
machine, having its visual identity
matched by an unmistakable sound from
the Double Mamba turbo-props.
   The type served in the anti-submarine
role from 1955 to the late 1960s, and
between 1960 and the 1970s undertook the
Airborne Early Warning (AEW) role. This
aircraft, XG797, served with HMS *Centaur*
in No. 870 Squadron, Fleet Air Arm.

image. The Venom's wings fold some distance from their roots. The central fuselage pod thrusts forward from the wings as they fold over its back, the slender twin booms a reminder of its precursor, de Havilland's first jet aircraft, the DH100 Vampire.

My drawing of the DH C24 Autogiro stands alone to represent the Rotary wing type. A very curious machine and difficult to draw, it has short-span wings and a tricycle undercarriage. To my eye, its appearance suggests its transitional state, somewhere between the aeroplane and the helicopter. If you think parts of this machine seem familiar, the design used the cabin of a DH 80A Puss Moth and the engine is from the famous DH Gipsy III. The C24 was

A touch of sea and land – De Havilland Vampire FB Mk 6 with the Sea Venom in the background. The Vampire was a breakaway from tradition for De Havilland. It has a centre pod designed round the DH Goblin jet engine and twin tail booms. This aircraft was delivered to the Swiss Air Force in April 1948.

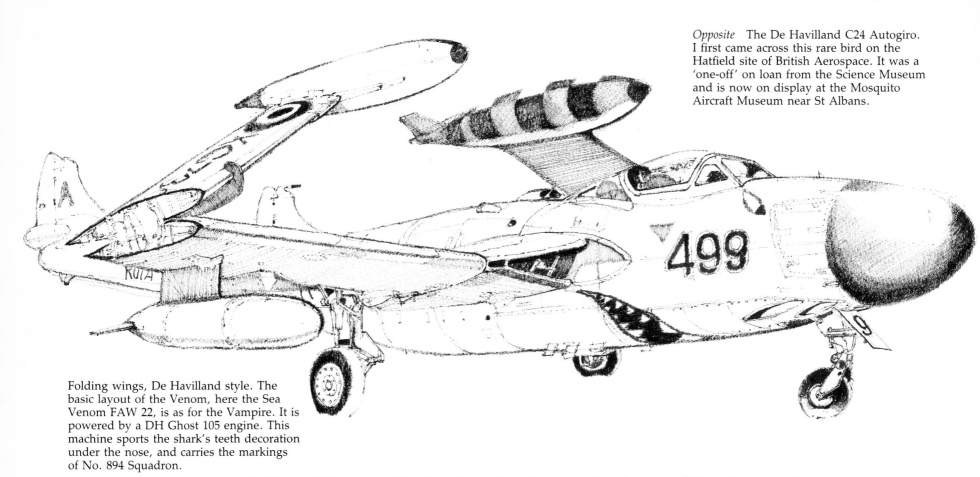

Opposite The De Havilland C24 Autogiro. I first came across this rare bird on the Hatfield site of British Aerospace. It was a 'one-off' on loan from the Science Museum and is now on display at the Mosquito Aircraft Museum near St Albans.

Folding wings, De Havilland style. The basic layout of the Venom, here the Sea Venom FAW 22, is as for the Vampire. It is powered by a DH Ghost 105 engine. This machine sports the shark's teeth decoration under the nose, and carries the markings of No. 894 Squadron.

built in 1931 by de Havillands at Stag Lane to the design of Don Juan de la Cierva, whose company provided the rotor assembly.

The wing is a tease to draw, for, with the exception of a plan view, it is always foreshortened by perspective. Because of this its apparent shape changes greatly with one's viewpoint. For the same reason, the dihedral – the degree of tilt through which the wing is lifted from its root to its tip – complicates matters even more and unwanted distortion may creep into the drawing.

It seems to be an inescapable fact that certain aeroplanes are more difficult to get right on the sketch pad than others. For example, the Mosquito wings appear to be too short when drawn from the three-quarter frontal aspect. I have often had to photograph the machine and make a comparison with this and my drawing to convince myself that the drawing is accurate. I find that both drawing and photograph look wrong! The Spitfire's wings are so subtle that even the thickness of a pencil line will make all the difference. Often, in a hangar, I have, because of restricted space, to sit closer to my subject than I would ideally choose to do. This may cause further problems of distortion since when you sit too close to an object and attempt to draw it, the final result often looks like the work of a fish-eye lens and the machine in the drawing is unrecognisable. These more technical aspects of drawing are what gives the process such a fascination. Of course one can take certain liberties such as using an artificial horizon, but usually I prefer to leave this to the pilot!

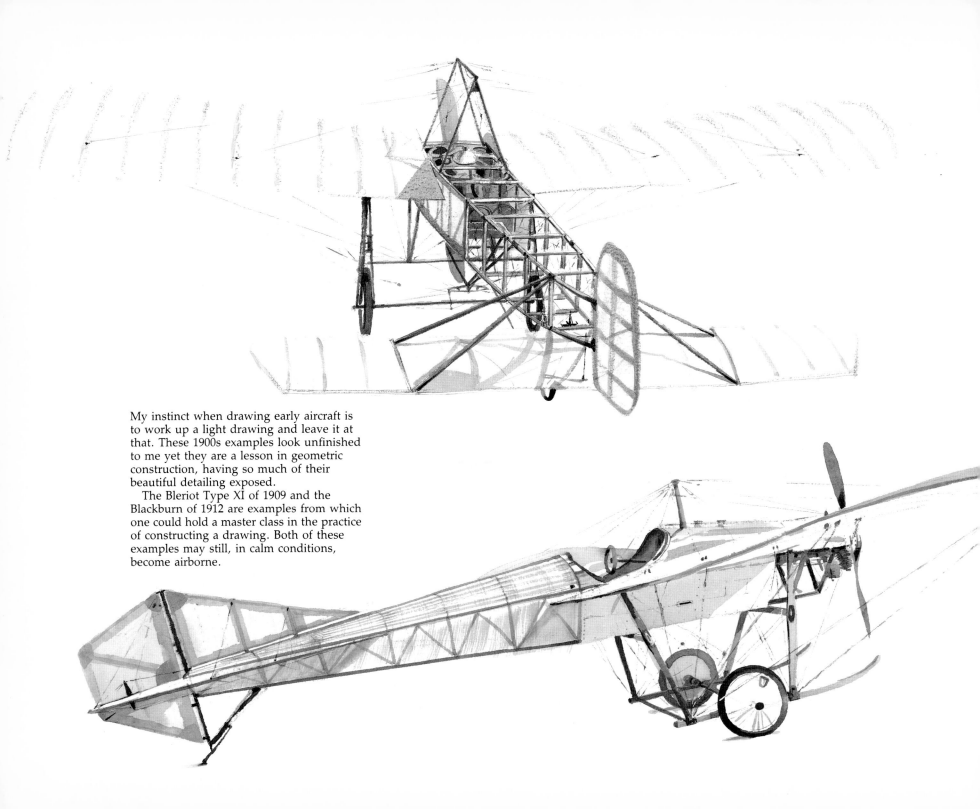

My instinct when drawing early aircraft is
to work up a light drawing and leave it at
that. These 1900s examples look unfinished
to me yet they are a lesson in geometric
construction, having so much of their
beautiful detailing exposed.

The Bleriot Type XI of 1909 and the
Blackburn of 1912 are examples from which
one could hold a master class in the practice
of constructing a drawing. Both of these
examples may still, in calm conditions,
become airborne.

The Fuselage

Technically the early flying machine was extremely basic; it had none of the sophisticated controls of a modern aeroplane. For the artist, however, the old machine – a skeletal apparition of sticks and wires – is much more complicated than its present-day counterpart, which is visually made up of simple shapes, of basic tubes and boxes.

The fuselage can be particularly tricky to draw since it is often only partly dressed – you can see right through it to the landscape beyond! There are complicated web-like structures interwoven with bracing wires apparently going everywhere, and as you can see through the framework to the other side you have to draw everything twice! – it matters not where you choose your viewpoint. Add to this the wings, tail and elevators (sometimes at the front!) and you have to look very hard indeed to understand what goes where. Of course I would not dream of calling it a lash-up, just as I refuse to regard an early car as an old crock; at first glance, however, there is at least an element of capriciousness about it!

Fortunately for the artist (and for the pilot) things did not stay that way. In the course of time the fuselage came to be covered, partially at first, then completely. All was no longer revealed. The aeroplane was fully dressed!

Much of my enjoyment in drawing an old plane is derived from a careful study of its construction – indeed, just as in the life class, if you know what lies beneath the skin you are able to draw your model much more convincingly. So, study its anatomy first. Take a look at the Bristol F 2b (1917) fighter as an example. It is fully covered, but if you have done your homework thoroughly most of its construction remains traceable, thinly disguised beneath the outer fabric. By now though, the engine is clothed by a metal cowling.

Bristol Boxkite. Reproduction of the original design of 1910, by F. G.
Miles Ltd at Shoreham, for the film *Those Magnificent Men in their
Flying Machines*

Having dressed the flying machine, the designer set about its development
apace. Aircraft development takes one of two main forms, the gradual refine-
ment and modification of an established theme and the voyage of exploration.

The Hawker Hurricane typifies the former. Stemming from a line of famous
Hawker biplanes, the Hurricane was the logical conclusion of a traditional
theme. The top wing has gone, the undercarriage tucks up underneath; the
famous biplanes are behind, but only just. The Hurricane was the new-look
monoplane with traditional underpinnings – a half-way house.

To examine a Spitfire fuselage is, by comparison, to leap into the new world.
With competition in its ancestry (the Schneider Trophy) the Spitfire fuselage
emerged as a true monocoque, a principle of unit construction that was a mile
away from those early machines with their open framework, bracing wires and
canvas-clad wings. To me the fuselage of a Spitfire is as beautiful as the wings;

A rugged construction is apparent on close
examination of the Bristol F 2b of 1917. Although
by this time aircraft tended to be fully clad, their
construction remained obvious. The introduction of
metal is of note on the engine cowling but the
greater part of the airframe remains fabric-covered.
It has the beginnings of a swivel turret in the form
of a scarf ring upon which a Lewis gun is mounted.
A second Vickers gun was synchronised to fire
through the propeller.

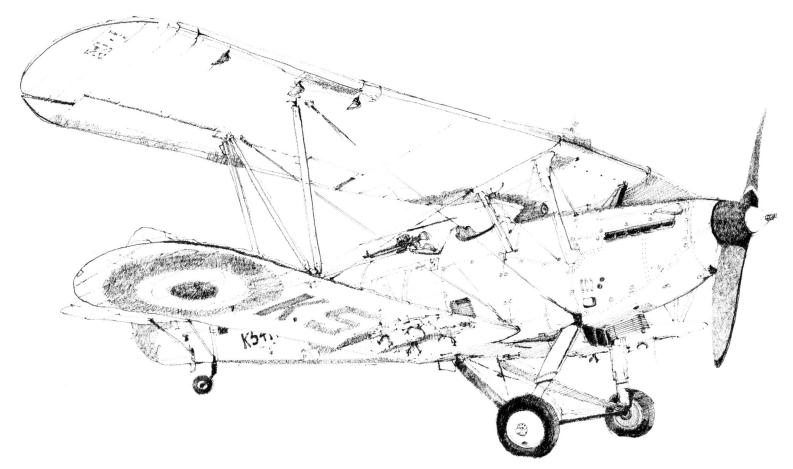

Hawker Hind, 1934. This is the drawing from which I made the painting on page 2. The Hind is a magnificent aircraft to draw. It has wonderful polished aluminium around the nose contrasting with fabric on the aft fuselage and wings. The shape is interesting too, since it looks both backwards and forwards; backwards because it is a biplane, a member of that illustrious family, Hart, Demon, Fury, etc; forwards, since I was constantly reminded of that most famous family member to come, the Hurricane monoplane, ghosted just beneath its skin.

This machine was delivered new to the Royal Afghan Air Force in 1938. Many years later it returned to the UK when it was presented to the Shuttleworth Collection, and this time it made the 6000-mile journey over land. After painstaking restoration in the Old Warden workshops, however, it flew again on 17th August 1981.

Hawker Hurricane Mk IIc. Although the Hurricane
was by no means the end of the line for the
renowned name of Hawker, it did embody the final
masterstroke to emerge from that unmistakable
former line of biplanes. Still partially fabric-skinned,
the machine is a delight to draw, since it embodies
the transition from old to new.

LF 363 was built at Langley in 1943 and is the
founder member of the Royal Air Force Battle of
Britain Memorial Flight.

The opposition. Focke-Wulf Fw190 and Spitfire Mk IX. When the Fw190 was first introduced in the summer of 1941 it could outfly the current Spitfire V, causing the Rolls-Royce Merlin to be enlarged to the more powerful '61' engine introduced in the Spitfire Mk IX. I drew the Spitfire at Booker Aerodrome. It has since featured in the video film *Spitfire*. The Fw190A–8/U1 is the more unusual twin-seat trainer version in the RAF Museum.

Wooden Wonder. Drawing used for the painting on page 14

I particularly like the nose – it has just room enough for the massive Merlin engine, its vee-formation cylinders squeezing their camshafts under two subtle bulges; while at the other end it tapers very gently towards its slim tail section. I think the best way to appreciate the finer points of the design is with the aid of a sectioned plan.

One of the great opponents of the Spitfire was the Focke-Wulf 190 of which the prototype was flown in 1939. The FW 190 was designed by Kurt Tank and, like the Spitfire, it was continuously developed, with 20 000 machines produced during the period of the war. One of these is now in the RAF Museum, where I was able to study briefly the type's slim-lean build. It is a small aircraft, with a span of 34 feet 5½ inches and a length of 29 feet. Even in the unusual twin-seat variant drawn, the fuselage is very impressive in its economy of build. It is far more a contemporary of the Spitfire in design terms than the Hurricane.

An entirely original way of producing a monocoque was employed to brilliant effect on the DH 98 Mosquito: the fuselage was made in two separate halves formed over concrete moulds and glued together. Of course my drawings of the Mosquito cannot show any of this, indeed, so smooth are the contours that an artist could almost persuade himself to believe that this fish-like form was carved from the solid.

More geometry. Geodetic construction of the rugged Vickers
Wellington bomber

Douglas C–47 Dakota. 43–15509 was drawn at Duxford. It is thought
to have taken part in Operation Overlord – the invasion of
Normandy in June 1944.

Geodetic construction was another innovation affording great advantages in weight-saving and offering outstanding advances in strength. Described in a wartime publication as a pair of spiral frames running in opposite directions and joining together at all points of intersection, and the finished result looking rather like a latticework fence. This technique was used first by Vickers for the Wellesley, which established a world distance record in 1938 for flying non-stop 7158.5 miles from Ismailiya in Egypt to Darwin in Australia, and later for the twin-engined Wellington. Unfortunately there are, to my knowledge, no flying examples of this highly original plane anywhere in the world. The war-time publication mentioned above – *The Book of the Wellington* – has a photograph of a line of Wellington carcases under construction 'somewhere in England', and it is this picture that I have used for reference for my drawing. Since the Wellington's basketwork structure of duralumin was very much associated with Sir Barnes Wallis, one can only reflect that it was after all he who earlier had designed the structure for the rigid airship R100; a frame structure therefore was a familiar path to develop.

The Douglas Dakota – DC–3 is one of a select band of immortal aircraft. It first flew in December 1935 and its military version, the C–47 flew on almost all fronts during the Second World War before going on to take part in the historic Berlin Airlift and the Korean and Vietnam conflicts. The 'Dak' is one of those examples of design that simply look right. There is not a line to be altered or a curve redrawn. It is quite simply 'right'.

An aeroplane with which I have a particular fascination and return to again and again is the very beautiful DH 89 Rapide. One of my chosen viewpoints is a three-quarter front with my customary low eye level. From here I have a view up to and through the canopy. Through the transparent panels I see the structure as it curves gracefully from the box-section cabin and over the cockpit down to the pointed nose. A superb subtlety of form and line.

The joy of drawing a machine like the Rapide is, again, the tracing of its construction beneath the spruce plywood and fabric. Its whole form is logical in terms of the material chosen for its construction. I have read that great care was taken over the detail design; special fairings, for instance, were made to carry the fabric over the 'corners' of the fuselage. The Rapide is the epitome of elegance. To draw it, one has to be able to appreciate not only its simple lines but its subtleties. It is a model of beauty.

The amphibian is a rare breed. Its fuselage must also serve as a boat and the

De Havilland Dragon Rapide – G-AIYR at Hatfield
after extensive fitting-out in preparation for her
flight to Cape Town

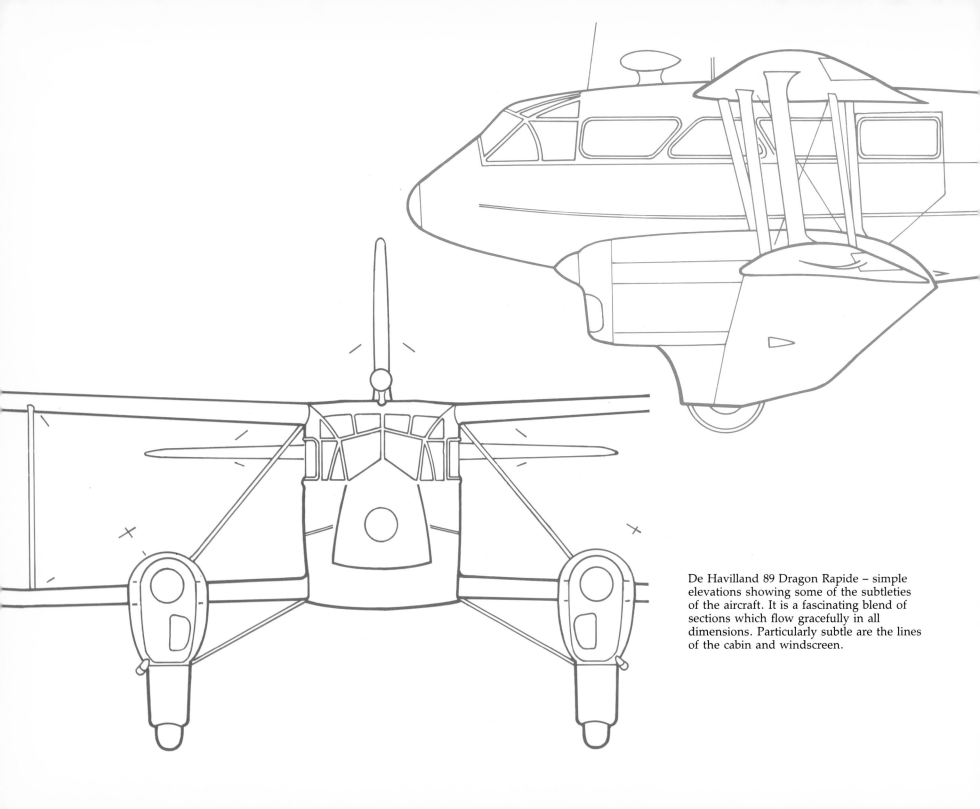

De Havilland 89 Dragon Rapide – simple elevations showing some of the subtleties of the aircraft. It is a fascinating blend of sections which flow gracefully in all dimensions. Particularly subtle are the lines of the cabin and windscreen.

description 'flying boat' is entirely accurate. Unlike a sea-plane, which has a conventional aircraft fuselage but floats instead of wheels, the flying boat may also have wheels. It therefore goes through a fascinating transition as the wheels are retracted on take-off from a metalled runway. The Catalina is a fine example. My drawing was made at Duxford aerodrome and therefore shows the type with the wheels in use. When flying with the undercarriage and the wing-tip floats retracted, the machine becomes very clean in form. The image of the Catalina is unmistakable. The features that particularly appeal to me are the subtle forms of the hull and the very curvaceous rear fuselage section. Since my first drawing of this example, it has been fitted out with side blisters and now looks very authentic.

When I first drew a 'heavy', (the term used during the war years to refer to a big aircraft) I was aware of a problem often encountered by people attempting to draw a large building, how to get far enough away from it to see the whole object at a glance. A four-engined aircraft is a vast object – cathedral-like in scale. It must seem like this to the crew members who become dwarfed as they approach it. I am fascinated to peer inside the fuselage – a mass of equipment and work stations with small metal seats.

The Lancaster impresses by the length of the bomb bay and by its load-carrying capacity. The Shackleton (*see* page 63), a maritime reconnaissance aircraft able to take a massive and varied weapon load, carries so much on-board equipment it really is a flying surveillance station – examined close to, it bristles with antennae; capable of long-duration flights, the fuselage must double as home for its crew. The Beverley is a cargo aircraft, a flying 'space'.

Opposite Consolidated PBY–5A Catalina. My time spent making initial sketches of the Cat was enhanced by an invitation to go aboard by a caring custodian who was washing her down by hand! Glancing over my shoulder from the cockpit, I was impressed by the sight of the two Pratt and Whitney engines high on the wing above my head.

The machine was flown to the UK from South Africa, landing at RAF Manston on 20th February 1985. It is now operated by Plain Sailing.

Below Avro Lancaster. Tail-end view of R5868, now at rest in the Royal Air Force Museum, after taking part in more than 120 bombing sorties

It impresses in terms of the massive bulk of its square-sectioned fuselage. A totally functional shape, it lacks any form of subtlety.

Looked at from an artist's point of view, these four-engined giants are really almost mobile buildings; when they move it is as though a building has been demolished, leaving nothing but a large empty space. When they fly, their size is diminished; they become plastic models, scaled-down versions of themselves. On the ground, however, the overwhelming impression is of size and bulk. They change the landscape where they come to rest. They are metal monsters.

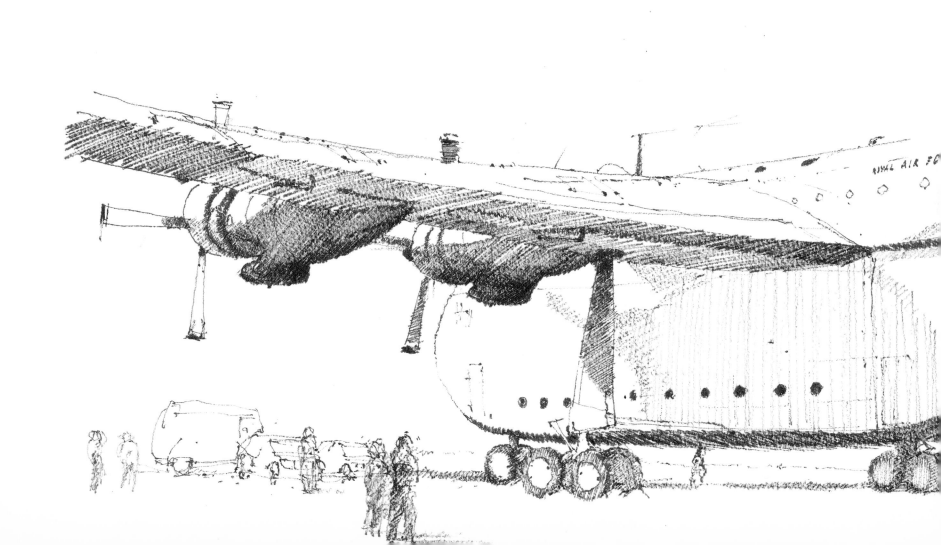

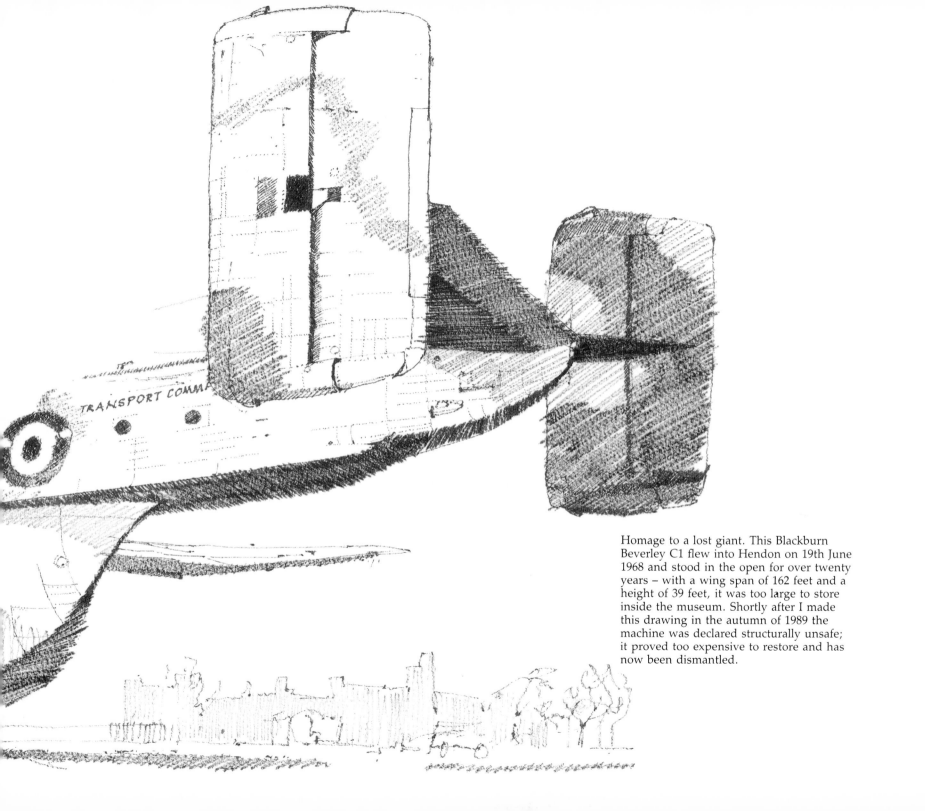

Homage to a lost giant. This Blackburn
Beverley C1 flew into Hendon on 19th June
1968 and stood in the open for over twenty
years – with a wing span of 162 feet and a
height of 39 feet, it was too large to store
inside the museum. Shortly after I made
this drawing in the autumn of 1989 the
machine was declared structurally unsafe;
it proved too expensive to restore and has
now been dismantled.

Shadows heightening the sleek lines of the
Grumman Tigercat F7F3. The type entered service
in 1944 but was too late to see active service; this
came later, however, when Tigercats were used in
the ground-attack role during the Korean War.

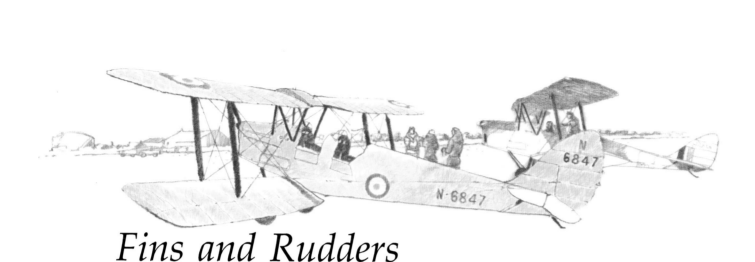

Fins and Rudders

The tail of an aeroplane may well emerge as its most striking feature. Certainly on the ground while the wing is always foreshortened by perspective, the tail fin is not. Examined along with other external features, the fin and rudder are to me a measure of style. It is a fact that however you care to argue the case along functional lines, some designers were consistent in producing good-looking aeroplanes on which the fin and rudder were particularly attractive.

Geoffrey de Havilland was outstanding in this respect. No matter what the purpose of the machine, the tail was unmistakable in its graceful elegance. Its silhouette seems to be made up of two simple curves, drawn from opposite points which meet at their apex. Three circles complete the shape.

The tail is without doubt de Havilland's visual hallmark. A corporate symbol which first appeared on the DH 3, (one of the large family of DH designs

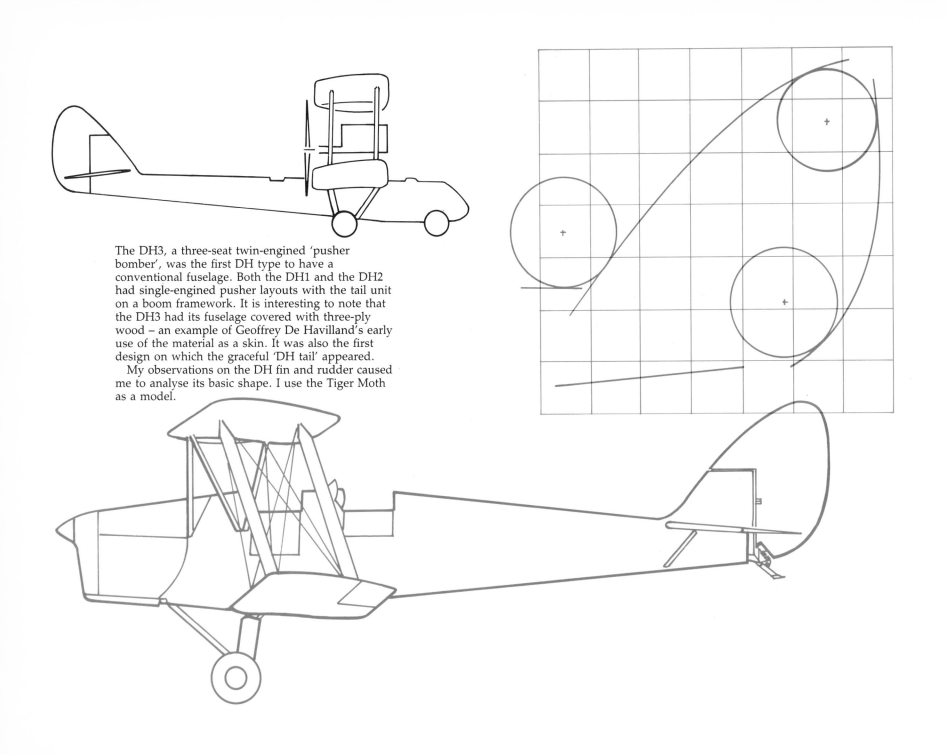

The DH3, a three-seat twin-engined 'pusher bomber', was the first DH type to have a conventional fuselage. Both the DH1 and the DH2 had single-engined pusher layouts with the tail unit on a boom framework. It is interesting to note that the DH3 had its fuselage covered with three-ply wood – an example of Geoffrey De Havilland's early use of the material as a skin. It was also the first design on which the graceful 'DH tail' appeared.

My observations on the DH fin and rudder caused me to analyse its basic shape. I use the Tiger Moth as a model.

Enjoying the Tiger Moth from a grass airfield

Spitfires on the flight line at Duxford –
three examples showing the development
of the fin and rudder to cope with the
increasing performance from the RR Merlin
and later Griffon engines
  The pencil drawing above is of a Mk Vc,
the clipped-wing variant. Removing the
wing tips improved handling at low altitude.

Large fin and rudder of the Westland Lysander

reviewed in *Flight* as long ago as January 1919), this shape persisted virtually unchanged throughout the twenties and thirties and is still recognisable on the Mosquito.

Tail shape may be a result of evolution, something created on the designer's drawing board and developed through a whole number of changes as a result of wind-tunnel testing or flying trials. I am fascinated by the account of the Spitfire tail detailed so fully in Dr Alfred Price's book. Apparently no fewer than five tails were tried and tested in the wind tunnel at Farnborough. I notice when I draw a Spitfire how its original very small fin and rudder were enlarged as the machine became more powerful. Structurally the tail of an aeroplane was usually similar to the wing and on early types supported by wire bracing. Even when this method had been superseded on the wing, the tail plane sometimes remained supported by a strut – the Messerschmitt BF 109 had this feature on many marks. I think it looks out of place on an aircraft having a fully cantilevered wing.

One of my fascinations is with the twin-boom layout. The basic idea of the boom principle appears quite early on. In the First World War, for example, de Havilland designs were of this configuration. It had an advantage for the two-

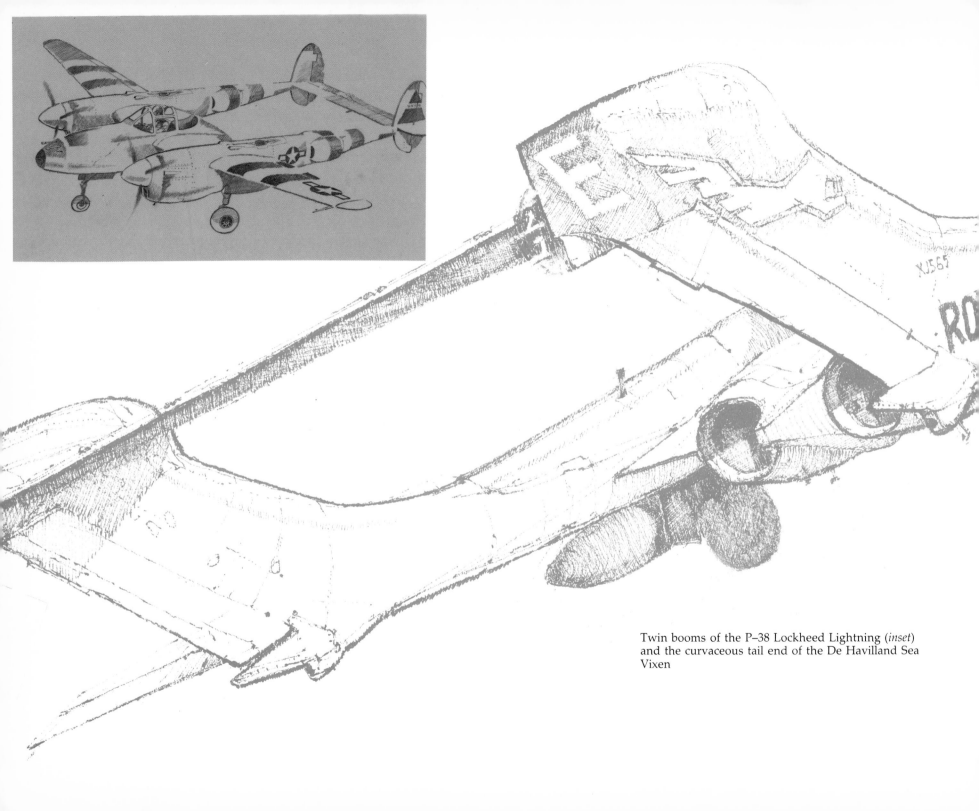

Twin booms of the P–38 Lockheed Lightning (*inset*) and the curvaceous tail end of the De Havilland Sea Vixen

seat scout machine favoured at this time in that the observer/gunner could be placed in the nose of the aeroplane where his view forward would be uninterrupted. The engine was placed in the rear, behind the pilot, its propeller pushing rather than pulling the machine along. The twin booms held the tail. This principle was utilised by a number of designers and appears again in the Second World War with one of the most well known designers of the period – the superb P–38 Lockheed Lightning, an aircraft that earned a fine reputation for its rugged construction. Its layout placed the two 1150 hp liquid-cooled Allison engines conventionally in front of the leading edge of the wings, while the space in the booms aft of the engines carried the turbochargers.

Among other famous aircraft to have twin-boom arrangements were the DH series Vampire, Venom and Vixen jet fighters. On the Vampire and Venom the layout perfectly suited the installation of the single jet engine aft of the cockpit. With the later Sea Vixen, the centre pod expands to hold two engines and two crew members; the cockpit is offset and the navigator is tucked away inside the pod. The fins form the tail end of the dramatic array of curved forms that make up the aircraft's silhouette. They remind me of my set of French curves. I think the entire machine must have been drawn up with the help of these drawing aids – it appears to me to be 'over the top' and very reminiscent of an American car of the sixties. However, it was a high performer in its day and could reach Mach I in a dive.

The Gannet, my favourite example of flying architecture, has two small fins acting as outriggers to the very large central fin. They probably provide extra directional stability at low speeds but visually they appear as the designer's final touch of abnormality, a cruel afterthought.

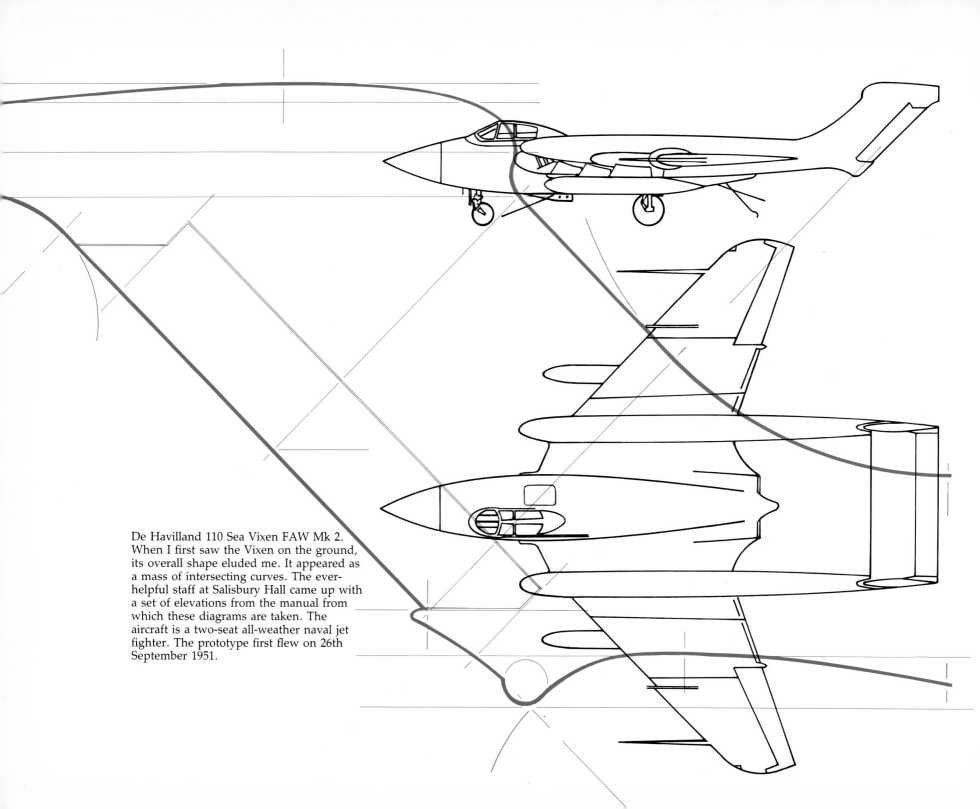

De Havilland 110 Sea Vixen FAW Mk 2.
When I first saw the Vixen on the ground,
its overall shape eluded me. It appeared as
a mass of intersecting curves. The ever-
helpful staff at Salisbury Hall came up with
a set of elevations from the manual from
which these diagrams are taken. The
aircraft is a two-seat all-weather naval jet
fighter. The prototype first flew on 26th
September 1951.

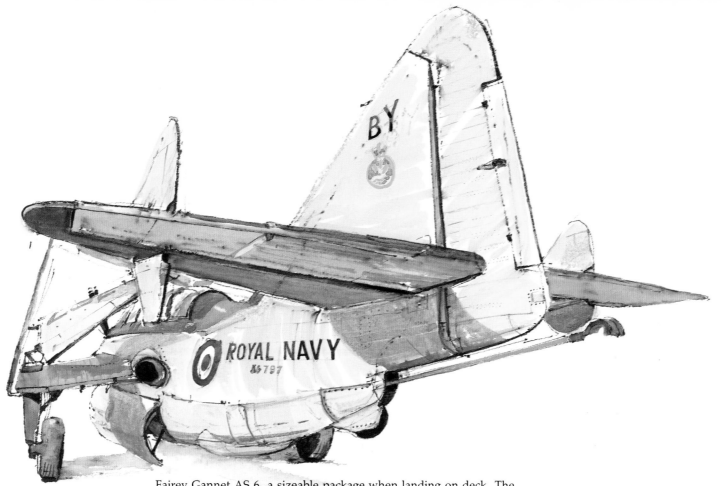

Fairey Gannet AS 6, a sizeable package when landing on deck. The machine had an empty weight of 15 069 pounds and a loaded weight of 19 600 pounds.

I am, of course, aware that sound reasons exist for a particular machine to have one, two or even three tail fins; their number, layout and eventual shape must relate to particular operational requirements and have close regard to the type's purpose in life. These requirements do not seem to be associated with a common scale or size, however. Looking through my folio I note that there is a great variety of machines featuring similarly shaped fins – the little Beech

Beechcraft 18 Expeditor – a lovely little aircraft with egg-shaped fins
designed as a communications machine. This specimen has an
immaculate aluminium finish.

Expeditor of 1937, for example, typifying for me that generation of small and
medium sized airliners produced by American companies like Lockheed, and
on the other hand, the massive B17 Fortress, typical of Boeing, with its unmistakable huge single dorsal fin pointing skywards. When I drew the Avro Lancaster, so well displayed in the Royal Airforce Museum, I deliberately chose to
draw from a three-quarter rear view, giving me the opportunity to draw those
huge egg-shaped fins which are a strong recognition feature. However, as I
drew I reflected again on the famous B17 Fortress; both after all, were heavy
bombers and both carried a large crew, yet very distinct and differing characteristics are evident – particularly in the chosen design of the tail unit. When I
visited Duxford to make my drawing of the Avro Shackleton I noted that Avro
had retained their preference, as they did for the earlier Lancaster, to design a
twin-tail layout, while Boeing continued their theme (on the B–29 and B–52)
with one large single fin and rudder.

I have in my library a little book entitled *Guide to Flying* written by S. E.
Veale, then (1942) on the staff of *The Aeroplane*. In this book Veale sums up the
state of the art of tails in days past in a way I find refreshingly amusing.

> They [the designers] can estimate and calculate the performance of the aeroplane they are designing to the last mile an hour in forward speed, and to the
> foot in the rate of climb, but they are never certain how the tail will behave.
> Many famous aeroplanes came into the world with a tail utterly unlike that
> with which they later won their laurels.

My own view is that of the artist, essentially romantic, though enquiring. It would be interesting to analyse aircraft shape as a graphologist does handwriting, to see what its nature reveals of the designer's character. What might Sir Geoffrey de Havilland's beautiful tails tell us about him? Surely the fin was his autograph.

Tails of many shapes and sizes – the Avro Shackleton MR3 and the B17 Flying Fortress

Shackleton XF 708 entered service with 201 Squadron, Coastal Command, in 1959. During subsequent years it saw service with 203 Squadron in Northern Ireland and in Malta. It was flown into Duxford in August 1972.

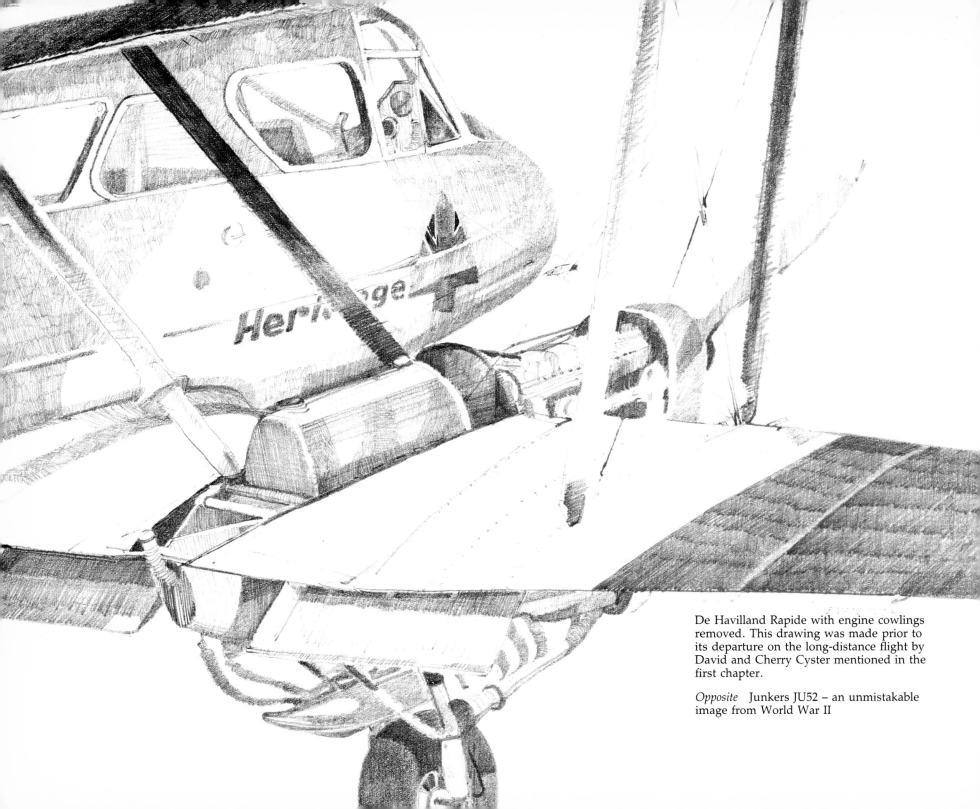

De Havilland Rapide with engine cowlings removed. This drawing was made prior to its departure on the long-distance flight by David and Cherry Cyster mentioned in the first chapter.

Opposite Junkers JU52 – an unmistakable image from World War II

The Engine

Read a few sentences about engines and you will become immediately involved in cubic capacities, horsepowers and the pros and cons of carburation versus fuel injection. To talk of engines purely from this technical aspect is for me entirely unsatisfactory. Can you image discussing a Rolls Royce Merlin in terms of horsepower alone? Figures tell the story of its development (almost twice the power was eventually achieved in the course of its long life – and it emerged as the Griffon). But, it is only when the machine is fired-up that the *sound* adds another dimension to our enjoyment, conveying its power and superb tuning better than any amount of technical data ever could. The very appearance, too, is impressive – as an exhibit removed from the airframe the Merlin reminds me of a swan, its two cylinder banks like the folded wings of this gracefully powered bird as it sits on the water.

I walked around the Science Museum's impressive collection of aero engines only half concentrating; determined though I was to go round the display in

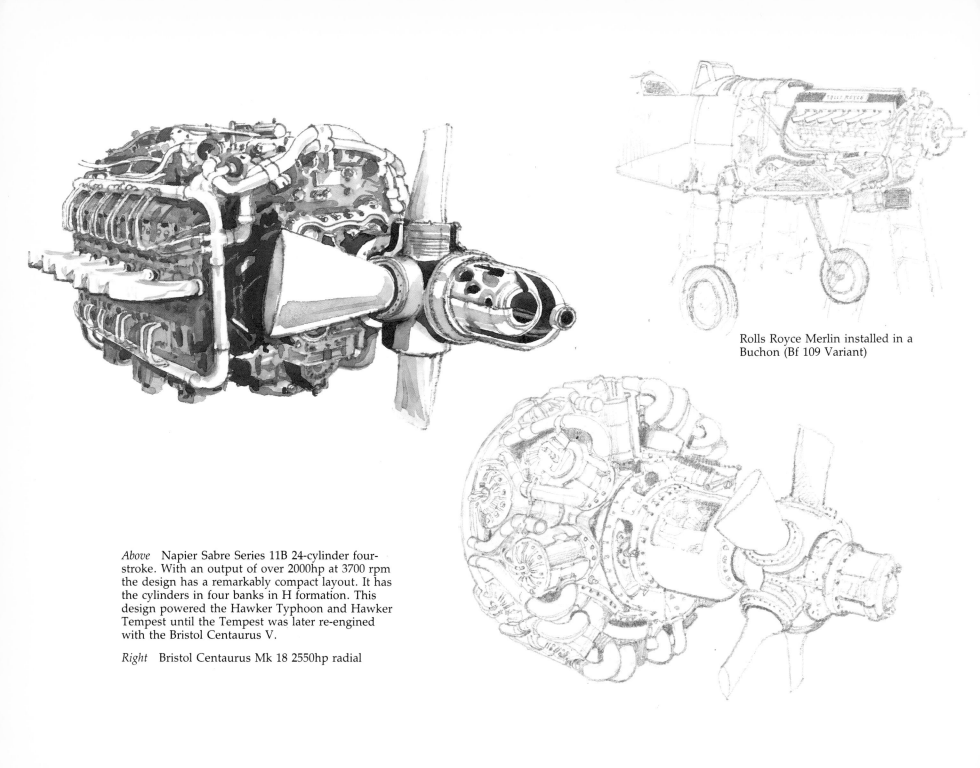

Rolls Royce Merlin installed in a
Buchon (Bf 109 Variant)

Above Napier Sabre Series 11B 24-cylinder four-
stroke. With an output of over 2000hp at 3700 rpm
the design has a remarkably compact layout. It has
the cylinders in four banks in H formation. This
design powered the Hawker Typhoon and Hawker
Tempest until the Tempest was later re-engined
with the Bristol Centaurus V.

Right Bristol Centaurus Mk 18 2550hp radial

historical sequence, I could not escape the constant draw of those huge machines of the Second World War.

The Napier Sabre is massive and squat. I wish I could hear the sound from those protruding exhaust stubs! Having its cylinders in an H-formation it was effectively two engines arranged one above the other, twenty-four cylinders cast in two blocks of twelve cylinders, in an upper and a lower bank. Two crankshafts were used. A mass of moving parts. Imagine the sound! The Napier Sabre was of course the standard power unit for the Hawker Typhoon and the early Tempest. The Typhoon was particularly renowned as a ground-strafing machine and carried heavy war loads of cannons and rockets.

To gaze at the symmetrical bulk of the mighty Bristol Centaurus is to behold one of the ultimate developments of the radial engine. Unlike the in-line engines, so familiar for their acceptance in the automobile world, the radial is quite different. With its circular layout it is impressively compact fore-to-aft. Having its cylinders exposed to the airstream, it has a wonderfully engineered appearance. The sound is every bit as identifiable as that from an in-line. You do not have to be a dedicated enthusiast to recognise the note from a pair of Pratt and Whitney Twin-Wasp radials before a Dakota comes into sight.

Having marvelled at a selection of the ultimate piston aero engines of the 1940s and 1950s, the sight of an early rotary is fascinating, but not exciting. To properly appreciate the rotary, you have to see one working. Until started it appears similar to a radial. It is only when it is fired up that you see that the whole thing rotates! The engine has its cylinders revolving around a stationary crankshaft, but you cannot do justice to this in a drawing. To my ear, the rotary makes a rather splashy sound, rather as though the cylinders were dipping into a saucer of milk! Physically these engines are quite small. However, to my eye, they have a purposeful look to them – they are altogether more appropriate for a flying machine than those early cumbersome in-line units.

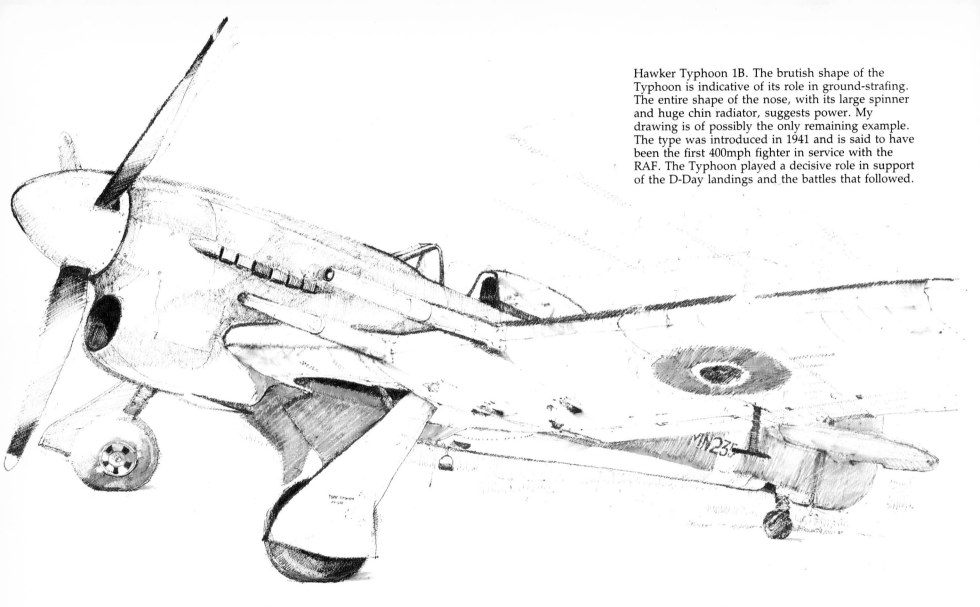

Hawker Typhoon 1B. The brutish shape of the Typhoon is indicative of its role in ground-strafing. The entire shape of the nose, with its large spinner and huge chin radiator, suggests power. My drawing is of possibly the only remaining example. The type was introduced in 1941 and is said to have been the first 400mph fighter in service with the RAF. The Typhoon played a decisive role in support of the D-Day landings and the battles that followed.

Most of the machines in my drawings use one or other of the three basic types of aero engine, namely the rotary, radial or in-line. There are variations, of course, the radial may be a double row (having its cylinders staggered), or

68

The Royal Navy Historic Flight's Hawker Sea Fury T20. I have depicted the aircraft as I saw her running up prior to take-off for a flying display – the entire machine was alive and vibrating under the power of the 18-cylinder engine. This example was the last but one T20 built, and first served with RNAS Anthorn, Cumbria, in 1951. Sadly it was totally destroyed after crash-landing with engine failure.

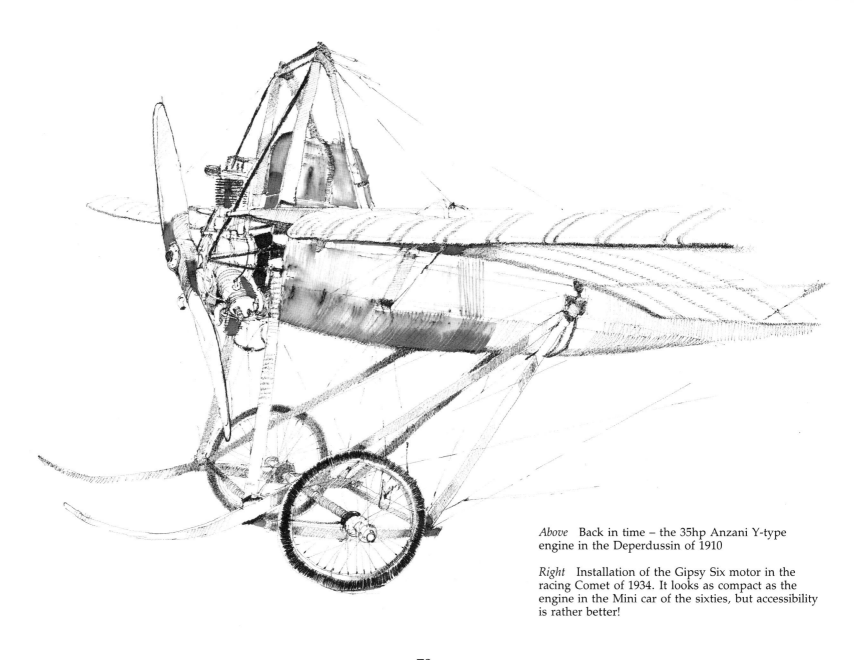

Above Back in time – the 35hp Anzani Y-type engine in the Deperdussin of 1910

Right Installation of the Gipsy Six motor in the racing Comet of 1934. It looks as compact as the engine in the Mini car of the sixties, but accessibility is rather better!

the in-line may be a V- or an H-formation. It is the variation of engineering design that makes the engine such a fascinating area of study. The advent of the jet engine changed things dramatically. For me the piston engine remains in both appearance and sound, the tamed monster that fires my imagination.

Apart from the obvious change in shape when more than one engine is used, the appearance of the single-engined type is influenced considerably by its power unit. Unlike a car, where the engine is tucked away out of sight, the aircraft is built around its engine. Of course on very early types you have to make an exception. On these old planes the construction was very reminiscent of a kite. To locate the engine you first look for the propeller! My drawings are principally of aircraft where the engine has a direct influence on the overall shape. Perhaps more accurately, I should include the air-intake and radiator installations, since these often influence the silhouette to a measurable extent.

With the radial engine things are usually straightforward. The engine calls for a large-diameter nose section and therefore the fuselage begins as a circular form. For example the Gloster Gladiator has a snub nose with the large-diameter nine-cylinder Mercury radial engine effectively dictating the form. The liquid-cooled SE5, however, has a very angular nose, the shape of which appears to

Top Gloster Gladiator, 1934, with 840hp Bristol Mercury IX 9-cylinder radial

Left Royal Aircraft Factory SE5a, 1917, with 200hp Wolseley Viper V8

Opposite Hawker Tomtit, 1928, with 150hp Armstrong-Siddeley Mongoose 111c 5-cylinder radial

be dictated more by the car-like, rectangular, radiator arrangement than by the V–8 Wolseley Viper engine.

It is interesting to see the advances designers were making by the late 1930s. With more power available, clean airflow was a necessity. Components were now being moved around in the interest of good streamlining. The Spitfire had exceptionally close-fitting almost 'tailored' cowlings around the Rolls Royce Merlin V12 engine. This was achieved to a large extent by placing the radiator layout under the wings. These under-wing 'boxes' eventually became an identification detail, progressively becoming bigger as the engine power increased; later marks of the Spitfire had two.

Of course it was not only the radiator that influenced the shape. Sometimes,

as with the DH Comet Racer, its air-cooled Gipsy Six engines were mounted inverted. This again gave a very clean line and economical frontal area to the cowling around the spinner. It also provided space behind the engines big enough to house the landing wheels when retracted.

There are designs which achieve remarkably attractive lines with radial engines and go against my general observations on the radial requiring a large circular section to the fuselage. One such example is the Hawker Tomtit, designed in 1928. It has an advanced steel-tubular constructed fuselage beautifully worked into a tapering nose in which is mounted a five-cylinder Armstrong-Siddeley Mongoose engine of radial layout. My diagram elevation of the frontal aspect of the aeroplane indicates the resulting pleasing line. To illustrate my remarks on the influence on shape of radiator position I have drawn two fighters from World War II in side elevation. Both have their character wholly influenced by the placing of the air intake.

The North American Mustang has a large 'belly' intake without which it would not be recognisable. This is a strong feature of identification and very apparent when the aircraft is being drawn in side elevation. Equally the Hawker Typhoon and Sabre-powered Tempest have shapes which are dominated in side and frontal aspect by their huge chin radiators. When later the Tempest was redesigned to be fitted with the Bristol Centaurus radial engine, it gained a completely new identity. Since the Hawker Sea Fury was similarly powered, my colour sketch on page 69 will provide a reasonable comparison.

Incidentally, the practice of 'customising' was surely started by our American cousins. Their aircraft in World War II were often emblazoned with strong graphic images and pin-ups, as indeed were our own bombers. The air intake, if in a convenient location, was an obvious mouth-like form. Hence the shark's teeth motif featured on many single-engined types. I can appreciate the temptation of such decoration, but I am amused by its apparent disregard for the

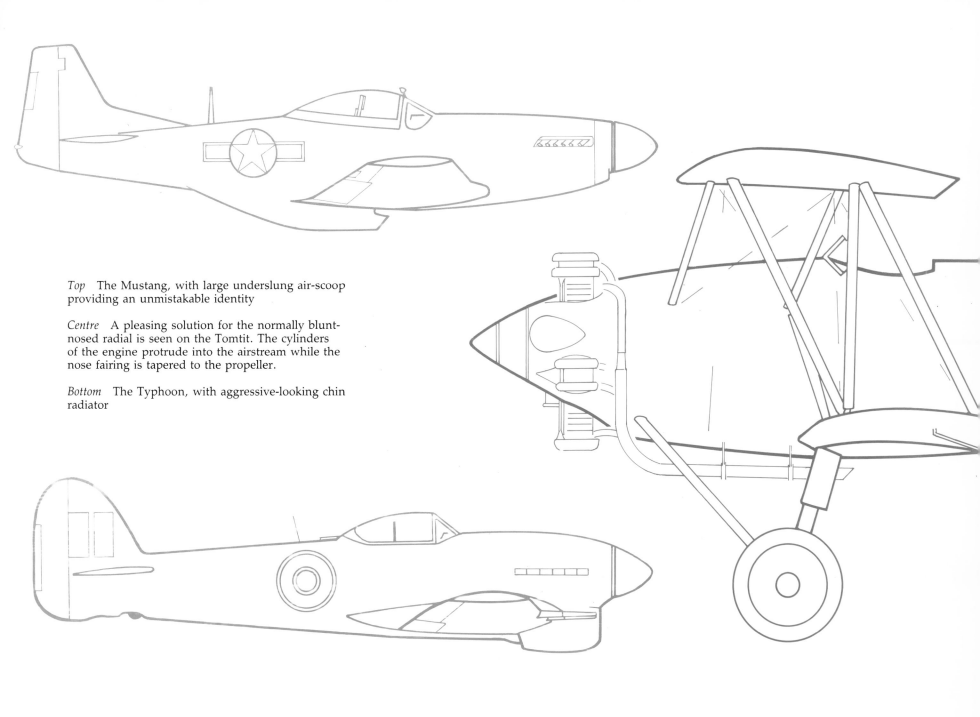

Top The Mustang, with large underslung air-scoop providing an unmistakable identity

Centre A pleasing solution for the normally blunt-nosed radial is seen on the Tomtit. The cylinders of the engine protrude into the airstream while the nose fairing is tapered to the propeller.

Bottom The Typhoon, with aggressive-looking chin radiator

As a study in colour and tonal contrast this Curtiss P40 Kittyhawk III makes an interesting drawing. The shark's mouth and spinner are well set off against the dull brown tones of the matt finish.

Specific instructions existed in the war years concerning markings, but many variations are evident. The personal customising of aircraft by individuals and squadrons ensured that the station 'artist' was kept busy!

careful camouflage of the aircraft on which it appears. Why bother to camou-flage if you are going to decorate your machine with brightly coloured symbols? It is an interesting use of shape though, a kind of three-dimensional mural.

Frequently we read of an aircraft having its performance greatly enhanced by the introduction of an improved propeller, and over the years this basically simple structure of two revolving blades has undergone tremendous develop-ment. The highly engineered variable pitch metal propellers of the Second World War assisted dramatically in the pilot's use of his engine's power and therefore the degree of control he had over his machine. With variable pitch it is possible to set the blades according to the performance required for different operating conditions. Often in wartime, for example, an engine would sustain critical damage and have to be shut down. When this happened the pilot could feather the blades and in so doing prevent the damaged engine from rotating as the propeller 'windmilled' through the airstream. The modern turboprop engine makes use of its propeller's reverse-pitch capability as an additional brake when landing – as one would expect a variable-pitch propeller has a very

This North American P–51D Mustang is privately owned and was drawn in the fighter hangar at Duxford. However, I wanted to see her as she might have appeared with the 357th Fighter Group, US Eighth Air Force based at Leiston on the East Suffolk coast.

Hawker Tempest V. High performance with superior wing gave this machine an advantage over its elder brother the Typhoon.

complicated set of gears in the hub, indeed, it has become a design study of growing importance . . .

. . . For me, however, as this folio demonstrates, allure lies in old aeroplanes, and I greatly treasure a splendid old wooden propeller I am fortunate enough to have in my possession. Dating back to around the First World War, and now covered in many layers of cracking varnish, it is beautifully constructed and beautiful to look at – the very embodiment of the craftsman's art.

When I draw a vintage piston-engine aircraft, I am intrigued by its propeller. As it stands on the ground, nose in the air, the propeller is often silhouetted against the horizon. It is an image I associate strongly with wartime airfields and particularly with those photographs taken at dusk. Gratefully, the sight remains to enjoy. I like to watch as an engine is fired up. A few hesitant turns of the prop, the sound of the first strokes and the puff of exhaust smoke, then the whole thing comes alive. Marvellous!

I have taken details from two drawings to visualise
this scene: in an air-field somewhere in England
Mosquito and Spitfire keep company.

Above Characteristic beam axle of the 1920s carried over to the next decade on the Hawker Tomtit

Opposite Perambulations of an early species – the Blackburn of 1912

80

The Undercarriage

Understandably since the aeroplane is first and foremost a flying machine, the majority of aviation artists depict scenes featuring aircraft in flight, perhaps a single plane depicted against storm clouds, or an air battle with numerous Spitfires and Messerschmitts locked in combat – the latter always seeming to come off the worst!

My approach is biased the other way. I like in the main to draw machines on the ground. In this condition, I can see them at first hand. Observe them in all their detail. Record how they are made.

Since my vantage point is usually a low one I have every opportunity to study along with everything else, the undercarriage – a real box of tricks. How ungainly the early undercarriages were! Take the Blackburn of the early 1900s for example – a framework attached to the airframe by long stork-like legs. The wheels are located on what amounts to a trolley base, and the entire assembly is braced with those familiar wires. A very geometric assembly, taking in the wings and fuselage, with those familiar skids protruding in front of it all. In fact it is this visually complicated arrangement that seems to date this particular monoplane which is otherwise to my eye, quite clean.

When I draw an aircraft of the 1920s, I am looking at design which remained

81

Two typically 1930s sporting aircraft, having contoured spats over their wheels

Left Miles Speed Six, 1935. Flown by Luis Fontes in the King's Cup Air Race of 1935

Below Percival Mew Gull, associated particularly with the famous pilot, Alex Henshaw, and in the record books for winning the 1938 King's Cup Air Race at 236.25 mph. In 1939 Mr Henshaw attacked the Cape Record. His total time on return to Gravesend was 4 days, 10 hours, 16 minutes – a record that still stands.

De Havilland Comet, wheels retracted

visually unchanged for many years. I have a mental picture of a typical 1920s aircraft: it has a fixed undercarriage, usually with that familiar 'beam' axle locating two bicycle-like wheels – you often see them rotating after the machine has taken off. At the tail is the familiar skid.

By contrast the 1930s saw streamlined forms for the first time, those curving shapes that got into architecture, product design and posters. Aircraft designers made good use of the trend. I am always attracted to the spat – that curvaceous cowling that partially covered the landing wheels – I ponder on how much advantage remained from the streamlined cowling after its extra weight had been taken into account. But in any case, it looked great. The little Mew Gull and the Miles Speed Six are typical.

The spat was carried through the war years and appears in contrast, for example, on the JU87 dive bomber and Westland's Lysander. Undoubtedly the real breakthrough was the introduction of the retractable undercarriage. Although there are examples around the 1920s (the Bristol Racer is one), my imagination is caught up again with the DH 88 Comet Racer. Although it was not alone in having retractable gear, its shape in the air was particularly pure because of it.

Interestingly, from my point of view as an artist, the folding undercarriage endows the aircraft with two identities. It is something of a shock to come face to face with a Mosquito at rest – such a clean and streamlined form in the air, so different on the ground! The Mosquito has a very complex undercarriage to draw. It appears to be made up of two main legs surrounded by a mass of

The complicated undercarriage design of the Mosquito makes a marked contrast to her remarkably clean lines when in flight. My studies for this machine were made at the Hatfield site, now part of British Aerospace. The serial number RR 299 is authentic, but the squadron code HT-E is not. It was applied for her role in the film *Mosquito Squadron*.

framework and bits of pipe. (Hardly a technical description, I know, but that's how it appears to me when I draw it!)

Interesting points of comparison come to view as I draw the Spitfire, Hurricane, BF 109 and FW 190. These machines vary in that the Hurricane has sufficient room and strength in its wings to allow the wheel assembly to pivot inwards, as does the FW 190; the Spitfire and BF 109, by contrast, have their wheels folding outwards, with the landing loads taken nearer the centre line. The BF 109 is narrow in the extreme, with pronounced negative camber. The two layouts have a very marked influence on these machines as they stand on the ground. The Hurricane has a much wider track and I am more aware of the metal covers partially obscuring the landing wheels. (*See* the painting on page 39.) An even greater contrast is provided by the Thunderbolt, whose massive bulk is well supported by the very wide track. Some aircraft look decidedly ungainly, either bandy-legged, or pigeon-toed! The Yak 11 advanced fighter trainer is an example of this, as is the otherwise sleek FW 190.

The tricycle undercarriage is, to me, mainly associated with American aircraft, at least until the 1950s. I think the Bell Series Cobras are typical of what I have in mind. Of course this layout offers significant advantages in ground handling but it lacks a certain drama I associate with the upturned nose of a 'tail-dragger'.

Undoubtedly, one of the biggest undercarriages was that belonging to the Short Stirling. Seen on the ground, it gave the machine a characteristic nose-up attitude which made it tower above all around it. Fighters were dwarfed by the size of the wheels and service crews could walk in safety under the propellers in the knowledge that they would not be chopped to pieces. The pilot sat on a level with a two-storey house so he was already airborne before take-off! As my friend testifies who flew these machines, they were a problem to taxi since the pilot sat well ahead of the two huge landing wheels. He relates how

86

Fw190 showing its wide-track undercarriage

Pictured at Duxford Aerodrome, the Bf 109 Buchon
of The Old Flying Machine Company. These flying
examples add real flavour to the Imperial War
Museum's own collection. I have drawn this
privately owned example along with other 'live'
aircraft that fly throughout the season. They include
a Corsair, two Mustangs and a resident Fortress. A
Spitfire flies overhead.

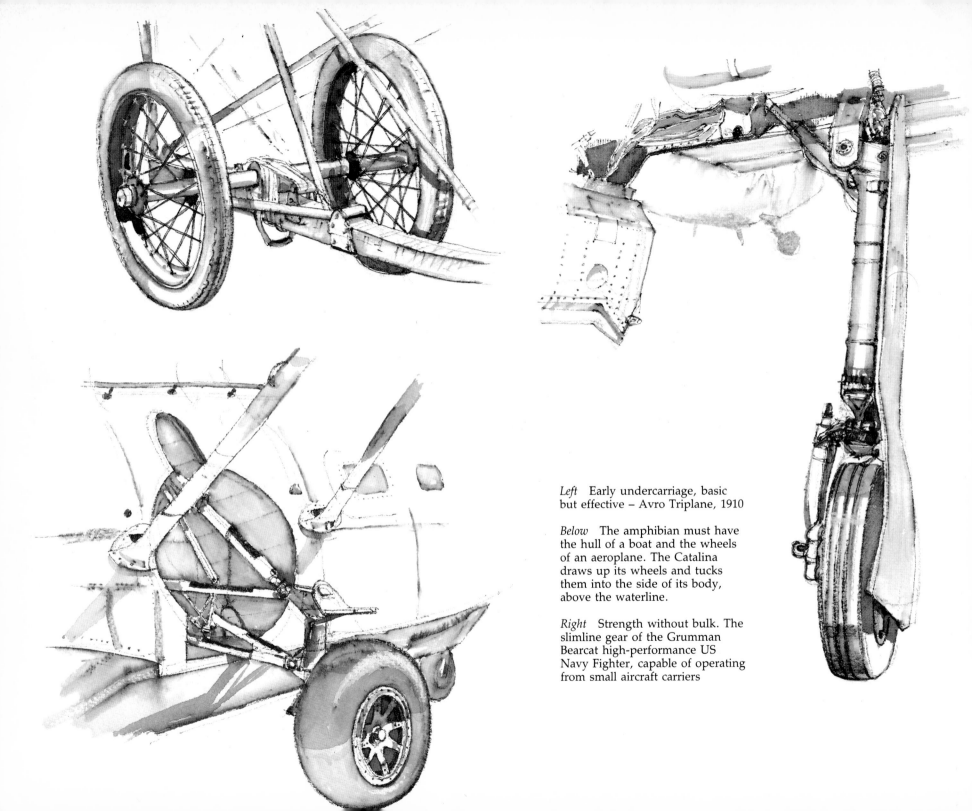

Left Early undercarriage, basic but effective – Avro Triplane, 1910

Below The amphibian must have the hull of a boat and the wheels of an aeroplane. The Catalina draws up its wheels and tucks them into the side of its body, above the waterline.

Right Strength without bulk. The slimline gear of the Grumman Bearcat high-performance US Navy Fighter, capable of operating from small aircraft carriers

Republic P–47 Thunderbolt. My original sketch for this painting
appears on the title page. Here I visualise the aircraft moments before
touchdown.

Right Yak–11 advanced fighter trainer. 'Fully aerobatic' was how this machine was described to me when I drew her at Booker Aerodrome – the wide-spread undercarriage is strictly a ground feature of this machine. Well respected for their outstanding performance as aerobatic machines, Yaks were also prominent as fighters, some 36 000 being built during World War II.

Below Bell P–63 Kingcobra. The tricycle undercarriage is a prominent feature of the type. The Russian markings on this example are in recognition of the large number of Cobras supplied to the Soviet Union in the war. On June 4 1990 the machine crashed shortly after take-off from La Ferte Alais, killing the well-known Duxford-based display pilot and Boeing 747 captain, John Larcombe.

Short Stirling Mk III. No complete example of this giant bomber remains for me to draw. This scene is based on photographs in my friend's collection. It depicts 'OJH' of 149 Squadron, RAF Methwold, receiving attention. She was brought down on the night of 1st June 1944 while mining off Knocke. The bomber was carrying a crew of seven, of whom the pilot was the sole survivor.

the tail gunner would let him know if the landing was not smooth since even with the main wheels on the runway the tail could be a full twenty feet above the ground – a long way to fall!

From my early childhood I have liked wheels. I would always check a toy to make sure the wheels rotated properly. Later, as a school boy, I still felt their fascination and maintained that they had a national character! During the Second World War I could recognise the difference between a German-manufactured wheel and a British one. I find today I continue to have this intuitive ability which is so difficult to rationalise but may have something to do with the stark functionality of the German war machine. As a school boy I didn't bother, I just 'knew'!

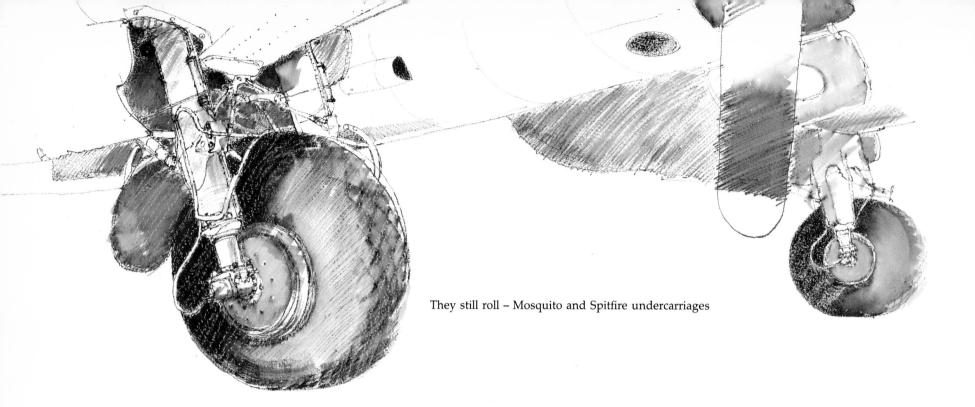

They still roll – Mosquito and Spitfire undercarriages

The undercarriage and wheels of an aircraft are studies in themselves. They have an individuality that gives a machine its particular stance. An unmistakable attitude as it sits on the ground. A second identity.

CONCLUSION

After compiling this collection of drawings from my folio I have tried to thread a brief text through them. I hope my words will reveal something of the pleasure I experience when I draw. I regard the aeroplane first simply as an object to be depicted. I am, however, since I suspect there is something of the engineer lurking within me, given a second appreciation, an appreciation of construction. This causes me to question – why is it made that way? I then have to combine my artistic appreciation of the given object with my enquiry into its construction – what does this amount to? I think it is a question-and-answer format – the interface between the process of design and manufacturing techniques on the one hand, and the artist delighting in the magnificent image that stands before him on the other. This leads to a desire to analyse that image as I draw it, to take it apart and to delight in its component parts – in some instances to want to possess them as the lover of the antique will treasure an artifact.

To say that an aircraft is built entirely on functional lines does not satisfy me – the Spitfire was designed wholly as a machine of destruction yet it is a beautiful object, a sculptor could not have created a more pleasing line and form. It is a masterpiece.

To satisfy my enthusiasm, I like to draw 'live' from my subject; I may take photographs as a back-up, but they are always 'second hand'. I prefer to be able to touch my subject, to experience it as my model. This is why most of my drawings are of machines at rest. My chosen medium is a clutch of pencils or a felt-tip pen. These are the most suitable, particularly when my vantage point is on a windy airfield.

Back in the comfort of my studio, I may choose to work up a drawing in colour – I prefer water colours with the odd pastel. While this process is going on my imagination may take over – a wheel may lift from the ground as for take-off or landing. Or perhaps a propeller will start to turn. My fantasies are at work – did I hear the sound of a Merlin?

The Aircraft

Note There may be variations in detail, particularly engine power, as aircraft are restored or modified.

Bibliography

Bishop, Edward (1980) *The Wooden Wonder*. Airlife Publishing Co Ltd, Shrewsbury.

Chant, Christopher (1987) *Aviation, an Illustrated History*. Black Cat, an imprint of Macdonald & Co (Publishers) Ltd, London.

Freeman, Roger (1978) *Thunderbolt – a Documentary History of the Republic P–47*. Macdonald and Jane's, London.

Gomersall, Bryce B. (1987) *The Stirling File* (revised edition). Air-Britain (Historians) Ltd, Tonbridge.

Gunston, Bill (1980) *Aircraft of World War 2*. Octopus Books Ltd, London.

Hardy, M. J. (1984) *De Havilland Mosquito, Super Profile*. Haynes Publishing Group, Yeovil.

Howe, Stuart (1984) *Mosquito Portfolio*. Ian Allan Ltd, London.

Lumsden, Alec (1974) *Wellington Special*. Ian Allan Ltd, Shepperton.

Munson, Kenneth (1980) *Aircraft of World War II*. Ian Allan Ltd, Shepperton.

Ogilvy, David (1982) *The Shuttleworth Collection*. Airlife Publishing Co Ltd, Shrewsbury.

Price, Alfred (1982) *The Spitfire Story*. Jane's Publishing Co Ltd, London.

Riding, Richard (ed.) (1981) *De Havilland – The Golden Years 1919–1939*. IPC Transport Press Ltd, Sutton.

Riley, Gordon (1983) *Vintage Aircraft of the World*. Ian Allan Ltd, London.

Veale, S. E. (1942) *Guide to Flying*. English University Press Ltd for Temple Press Ltd, London.

Periodicals

Fly Past, edited by Ken Ellis, is published monthly by Key Publishing Ltd in Stamford, and distributed by IPC Magazines.

Aeroplane Monthly, edited by Richard Riding, is published monthly by Prospect Magazines, a division of IPC Magazines, and distributed by Quadrant Publishing Services.

Official Museum Guides

Imperial War Museum, Duxford
The Royal Air Force Museum, London
Battle of Britain Memorial Flight 1990, London (50th Anniversary Edition)
The Royal Navy Historic Flight, RNAS, Yeovilton

Video

Spitfire written by Brian Johnson, produced by Garry Pownall, published by Thorn EMI Video Limited, 1983.

In memory. Remains of the concrete moulds around which the mighty Mosquito was formed rest among spring flowers at Salisbury Hall, March 1990.

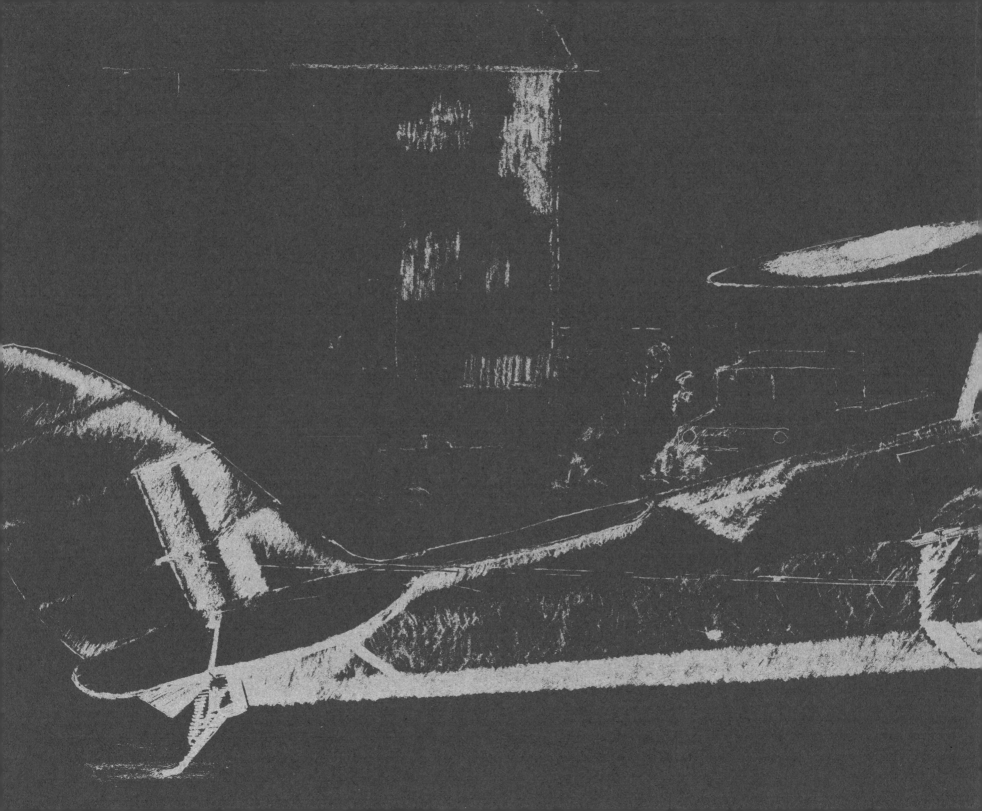